CW00375411

Computer users are not all alike.
Neither are SYBEX books.

We know our customers have a variety of needs. They've told us so. And because we've listened, we've developed several distinct types of books to meet the needs of each of our customers. What are you looking for in computer help?

If you're looking for the basics, try the **ABC's** series. You'll find short, unintimidating tutorials and helpful illustrations. For a more visual approach, select **Teach Yourself,** featuring screen-by-screen illustrations of how to use your latest software purchase.

Mastering and **Understanding** titles offer you a step-by-step introduction, plus an in-depth examination of intermediate-level features, to use as you progress.

Our **Up & Running** series is designed for computer-literate consumers who want a no-nonsense overview of new programs. Just 20 basic lessons, and you're on your way.

We also publish two types of reference books. Our **Instant References** provide quick access to each of a program's commands and functions. SYBEX **Encyclopedias** and **Desktop References** provide a *comprehensive reference* and explanation of all of the commands, features, and functions of the subject software.

Sometimes a subject requires a special treatment that our standard series don't provide. So you'll find we have titles like **Advanced Techniques, Handbooks, Tips & Tricks,** and others that are specifically tailored to satisfy a unique need.

We carefully select our authors for their in-depth understanding of the software they're writing about, as well as their ability to write clearly and communicate effectively. Each manuscript is thoroughly reviewed by our technical staff to ensure its complete accuracy. Our production department makes sure it's easy to use. All of this adds up to the highest quality books available, consistently appearing on best-seller charts worldwide.

You'll find SYBEX publishes a variety of books on every popular software package. Looking for computer help? Help Yourself to SYBEX.

For a complete catalog of our publications:

SYBEX Inc.
2021 Challenger Drive, Alameda, CA 94501
Tel: (510) 523-8233/(800) 227-2346 Telex: 336311
Fax: (510) 523-2373

SYBEX is committed to using natural resources wisely to preserve and improve our environment. As a leader in the computer book publishing industry, we are aware that over 40% of America's solid waste is paper. This is why we have been printing the text of books like this one on recycled paper since 1982.

This year our use of recycled paper will result in the saving of more than 15,300 trees. We will lower air pollution effluents by 54,000 pounds, save 6,300,000 gallons of water, and reduce landfill by 2,700 cubic yards.

In choosing a SYBEX book you are not only making a choice for the best in skills and information, you are also choosing to enhance the quality of life for all of us.

Windows Magic Tricks

Windows™ Magic Tricks

Judd Robbins

SYBEX

San Francisco • Paris • Düsseldorf • Soest

Acquisitions Editor: Dianne King
Developmental Editor: Christian T.S. Crumlish
Editor: Peter Weverka
Project Editor: Brenda Kienan
Technical Editor: Sheldon M. Dunn
Word Processors: Ann Dunn, Susan Trybull

Book Designer, Illustrator: Lucie Živny
Screen Graphics: Cuong Le
Typesetter: Dina F Quan
Proofreader, Production Assistant: Arno Harris
Cover Designer: Ingalls + Associates
Cover Photographer: Mark Johann

Screen reproductions produced with Collage Plus.

Collage Plus is a trademark of Inner Media Inc.

SYBEX is a registered trademark of SYBEX Inc.

TRADEMARKS: SYBEX has attempted throughout this book to distinguish proprietary trademarks from descriptive terms by following the capitalization style used by the manufacturer.

SYBEX is not affiliated with any manufacturer.

Every effort has been made to supply complete and accurate information. However, SYBEX assumes no responsibility for its use, nor for any infringement of the intellectual property rights of third parties which would result from such use.

Library of Congress Card Number: 92-61127
ISBN: 0-7821-1119-X

Manufactured in the United States of America

20 19 18 17 16 15 14 13 12 11
10 9 8

To Betty and Sheldon

acknowledgments

These people, who helped so much in the development and production of this book, would go unnoticed by the reading public were it not for this solitary book page. I am deeply indebted to Christian Crumlish for his creative input and constant inspiration; to Peter Weverka for a superb and thorough editing of the manuscript; and to technical editor Sheldon M. Dunn for a job well done. I would also like to thank Joanne Cuthbertson and Brenda Kienan for keeping the manuscript on track; Lucie Živny for her excellent book design; and typesetter Dina Quan, proofreader Arno Harris, screen graphics technician Cuong Le, and word processors Susan Trybull and Ann Dunn. Special thanks go as well to Richard Mills and Molly Spofford for always being on time, and of course to SYBEX'S acquisitions editor, Dianne King.

table of contents

introduction

This book is entertainment. Some of its programs do offer useful functionality for the Windows system, but even those programs were meant to be entertaining. You will enjoy yourself as you try them out. You will catch yourself smiling in some cases and shaking your head in amazement in others.

Sixty-one unique programs appear in the pages of this book and on the diskette bound to the back cover. The directory names are listed in the inside front cover along with a brief description of each program.

how the book is organized

The book is organized into four major Parts, each with a group of programs arranged in alphabetical order. The four Parts are

- **Smoke & Mirrors**, which contains programs that defy understanding. You'll wonder how these things are even possible.

- **Presto-Change-O**, which contains programs that will fill you with wonder. You'll be amazed by the things that can be done to your Windows system.

- **Spellbound**, which includes programs that are awe-inspiring. You'll sit for hours just watching the many colorful and eye-catching results of these programs.

- **Abracadabra**, which offers applications that will involve and engage you. You'll be a willing and enthusiastic participant in this group's witchcraft.

who this book is for

This book is for you if you use Windows at all. You can be a complete beginner and still enjoy and use every single program here. You can be the most sophisticated user of Windows around, and many of these programs will still bring a smile to your face. You'll enjoy seeing some, using others, and playing with still others.

This book collects in one place the most amazing, interesting, startling, entertaining, and wondrous set of magical Windows programs you've ever seen. You will discover tricks that you didn't realize were even possible. The book is written to be understood by every reader, regardless of his or her experience level. You only need to start a program to enjoy its capabilities. A later section of this Introduction explains a variety of ways to run these programs. Each chapter in the book explains how to use the programs once you've run them. The programs do fantastic things, but each is remarkably easy to run and use.

getting in touch with the authors

Each program in this book has an author. Except for some of the freeware programs, mailing addresses or electronic e-mail addresses are provided for reaching each author. I've included this information at the end of each chapter in a section called "Behind the Trick."

If you have comments, criticisms, or suggestions that relate to a particular program, please communicate with its author. If you'd like to get in touch with me, do so at

Judd Robbins
P.O. Box 9656
Berkeley, CA 94709
CompuServe: 70303,1670

Please feel free to write me with opinions about the programs I selected for this edition of *Windows Magic Tricks*. Tell me what you liked or didn't like, and why. Tell me what you'd like to see in future editions of this book. Maybe more of one type of program and less of another. I'm open to suggestions. Perhaps you'd like to suggest a completely different book with shareware of a different nature altogether that you'd like me to find for you.

Get in touch. Maybe you know of a program that you think should have been included. Let me know. A lot of very good software is being developed in the shareware world. I'll be glad to learn of entries for future compilations like this one.

If you're an author of a shareware product that I did not include here, write to me and send your current version. I'll be glad to consider it for a future revision, or a completely new version, of this book. Even if you're an author of one of the products already offered here, keep me apprised of new versions of your software and of products you may have written.

▫ ▫ ▫ ▫ ▫ ▫ ▫ using the magic trick programs

Windows offers a variety of ways to run executable programs. The programs in this book do many things, but each can be initially run in the same way. The following sections offer several alternative methods for running Magic Tricks. Choose the one that best suits your needs. You can even use more than one technique for the different programs. For example, you may want to run one or more of these programs automatically each time you start Windows.

None of the programs in this book are lethal. No viruses or data destroyers are included here. Nevertheless, I can't know in advance what mix of programs is running on your system when you run one or more Magic Trick programs. Common sense and cautious system management advise you to try out the magic tricks only when nothing critical or crucial is going on with your system. If you can't do this, back up all your important work before you try a Magic Trick application. Sometimes the interaction among Windows programs, both commercial and shareware, crashes the system or forces you to exit Windows and restart.

Most, but not all, the programs require Standard or Enhanced mode to execute successfully. Naturally, those are the only modes available in Windows 3.1.

▪ ▪ ▪ ▪ ▪ ▪ ▪ ▪ ▪ ▪ ▪ ▪starting an application

Suppose you've tested some of the Magic Tricks in this book and you'd like to create a representative icon for one of them. For example, one program in the "Abracadabra" section, called PINUP1O.EXE, provides the computer equivalent of those stick-em notes used in offices. Suppose you like this program and you want to give yourself easy access to it by way of an icon in a program group.

To create an icon for that program,

1 Select the program group you'd like it to be in.

2 Pull down the File menu and choose New Program Item.

3 Fill in the Description for the label below the icon, enter a Command Line (C:\SYBEX\PINUPS\PINUP10.EXE in our example), and select OK.

Presto, your icon is ready and waiting for you to choose it.

The StartUp program group is a special feature of Windows 3.1 and higher. Program icons included in the StartUp program group automatically run when Windows starts up. Earlier versions of Windows used special entries, such as Load= and Run=, in the WIN.INI file to control startup processing. These entries are still available (see below). In fact, some third-party programs actually install themselves on your system by making adjustments to one or both of these lines in your system's WIN.INI file. However, a StartUp group is easier to set up and maintain, so I recommend it for the Magic Tricks you want to run each time you start Windows.

But I only set up icons in the Program Manager for the few most commonly run Magic Trick programs. To run other, less frequently needed programs, I use different methods. To test new programs on my system, I simply pull down the Program Manager File menu, select Run, and type in the complete pathname to the program. Windows runs it for me by making the directory containing the program the default directory.

Finally, when I use the File Manager program, I can run programs in still more ways. I can choose the Run command from the File Manager File pull-down menu, which operates in the same way as the Run command in the Program Manager. Alternatively, when displaying a Directory Tree window, I can simply select any executable program name (EXE, COM, BAT, or PIF) and ask Windows to run it for me.

You can select and run a program from the File Manager by double-clicking on it. This is my favorite way to run Magic Trick programs. Alternatively, you can highlight the program name, pull down the File menu, and choose Open.

▫ ▫ ▫ ▫ ▫ ▫ ▫ running applications at startup

Windows 3.1 contains a built-in program group in the Program Manager called StartUp. When you create an icon in this group, or move or copy an icon into this group, the application it represents will be run automatically when you start up Windows. This is a convenient way to set up your desktop in a consistent manner each time Windows begins. Place the icons whose programs you use most often here so that they're immediately available to you when the Windows desktop first appears.

Former versions of Windows could create the same effect. They ran applications automatically by including their names on the Run= line of the WIN.INI file (in the [Windows] section). Whether they're in the StartUp program group (in Windows 3.1 only), or on the Run= line of a Windows WIN.INI file, the named programs will be started. The individual program's normal startup procedure will be followed at this point.

Some people like to initiate one or more application programs automatically when they begin Windows. It is possible. You needn't wait until Windows has begun to launch or run the applications via the File Manager or some equivalent launching program. Windows 3.1 users can enter a program's icon in the StartUp group of the Program Manager and its underlying program will run when Windows is started.

Users of Windows 3.1, as well as users of earlier versions, can also use another technique. They can use an editor, or SYSEDIT.EXE, or another means to change the LOAD= or the RUN= line in the WIN.INI file (it is found in the WINDOWS directory). You can initiate one or more programs by adding their names to these lines.

For example, to simply load both the Icon Calculator and the Pinup programs and make their icons appear at startup time, adjust the LOAD= line in the [WINDOWS] section of WIN.INI to read

LOAD=C:\SYBEX\ICONCALC.EXE C:\SYBEX\PINUP10.EXE

However, the automatic loading or running of programs at startup takes longer than not loading or running programs. In one respect, it's just a convenience to avoid having to initiate each program individually later on. But it still takes a finite amount of time. So, to minimize the overall drain on your system memory and resources, just load or run the programs that you want to be available all the time.

installing the applications

The diskette that comes with this book contains all the programs described in this book. The programs are in compressed format. The actual expanded size of the files comes to more than 3 megabytes.

To install all of the Magic Trick programs, you must have approximately 4.3 megabytes of free disk space. During the installation procedure, extra space is temporarily consumed in order to speed up the process. This space is automatically erased after the Magic Trick programs are decompressed. When the installation process is complete, your hard disk will have a SYBEX directory with 60 separate subdirectories. Most of the directories will contain a main executable program for one Magic Trick application along with its support files. Two of the subdirectories, BPUTILS and FUN, contain multiple executable programs. All of the magic tricks are described in detail in this book and briefly on the inside front cover.

Before you install the Magic Tricks, exit Windows or any other program you may be running. When you are at a DOS prompt,

1 Place the Magic Tricks diskette into a diskette drive.

2 Change to that drive.

3 Run the SYBEX batch file from the DOS command prompt. Specify your hard disk as the first parameter.

For example, to install all of the Magic Tricks onto drive C, you might place the diskette in drive A and type these two instructions:

A:
SYBEX C:

The SYBEX.BAT batch file controls the copying and decompressing of all the Magic Tricks programs from the single diskette onto your hard disk. SYBEX.BAT creates a \SYBEX directory and separate subdirectories for most of the Magic Trick programs. After you run

SYBEX.BAT, you will find nearly all the Magic Trick programs in subdirectories under the SYBEX directory on your hard disk. Because of special requests by authors, there are two exceptions. First, the BPUTILS subdirectory contains the CALPOP, FLIPPER, and RUNNER programs. Second, the FUN subdirectory contains a group of seven related and similar programs (BUGS, BURST, BURST2, EYES, FACE, FRIED, and WIZ).

After you've completed the automatic installation, start Windows by typing WIN and have fun trying out all the programs. You can erase programs that you do not wish to retain. Because they are conveniently organized in their own subdirectories, you can use the File Manager to quickly erase an entire directory and all its contents.

▪ ▪ ▪ ▪ ▪ ▪ ▪ ▪ ▪ ▪ shareware and freeware

The Magic Trick applications in this book are either shareware or freeware. The documentation that accompanies each application explains what each product is and how you may use it. It is important to understand the differences between commercial, shareware, and freeware applications.

Commercial applications typically are sold in stores or by mail order for a fixed price. The package contains a license to use the product, usually on a single computer, and has accompanying documentation.

Freeware programs have virtually no strings attached. They usually offer no restrictions on non-commercial use, although the author still retains the ownership, or copyright, of the program itself. Documentation is usually minimal. Public domain software is the extreme example of freeware. It is simply offered to the world with no restrictions on use of any sort, including repackaging or rewriting as a commercial product.

Shareware consists of products that are usually offered to the public in their complete, unrestricted form at no initial charge. Shareware distribution gives users a chance to try software before buying it. If you try a shareware program and continue using it, you are expected to register. Individual programs differ when it comes to the details of registration. Some politely request it and others require it through a programming mechanism, such as a maximum trial period after which the program no longer operates. After you register, you usually receive the simple right to continue using the software. You may also receive an updated program with a printed manual, or even the right to access the author's Bulletin Board system and receive future upgrades for free.

Copyright laws apply to both shareware and commercial software. The copyright holder retains all rights, with a few specific exceptions as stated below. Shareware authors are often accomplished programmers, just like commercial authors, and their programs are of comparable quality.

The main difference between shareware and commercial ware is in the method of distribution. The author specifically grants the right to copy and distribute the software, either to all and sundry or to a specific group. For example, some authors require written permission before a commercial disk vendor may even copy their shareware program.

Shareware is a distribution method, not a type of software. The shareware system makes fitting your needs easier, because you can try before you buy. And because the overhead is low, prices are low also. Shareware comes with the ultimate money-back guarantee—if you don't use the product, you don't have to pay for it.

A common technique for encouraging registration is for the program to display a dialog box that reminds you that you haven't yet registered. As a result, some users have renamed shareware "nagware." Usually, users receive a registration number that disables the shareware reminder notice when the program is started.

Non-registered users of the shareware included with this book are typically granted a limited license to make an evaluation copy for trial use. Use this copy to determine whether the program is suitable and desirable for continued use. At the end of the trial period, either register your copy or discontinue using the shareware program.

Registering has additional benefits beyond simply paying for the legal right to continue using the software. By registering each product, you can keep informed about future upgrades, with all included new features and any necessary bug fixes.

Please understand further that the purchase of this book does not constitute any form of payment of required registration or shareware fees to the corresponding software authors. All of the author's disclaimers of responsibility regarding their software creations still apply. Further, none of the shareware authors give up or transfer any of their ownership rights or copyrights to their software programs.

▪ ▪ ▪ ▪ ▪ ▪ ▪ ▪ ▪ ▪ don't panic—a disclaimer

The programs in this book are startling, striking, or distressing, depending on your mood and your level of Windows expertise. If something goes wrong, in nearly all cases you can shut down a Magic Trick program and remove its visual effects in the process. Follow these steps:

1   Display the Task Manager by pressing the Ctrl-Esc key combination.

2   Highlight the name of the offending, disturbing, or annoying program.

3   Select End Task.

4   Smile. Don't worry any more. Be happy.

In some cases the trick program hides itself even from the Task Manager. Several of the programs in Fun do this. In such cases, as I point out in the chapter, you'll either have to exit Windows or wait until the program displays a dialog box for closing it. In cases where the screen display is temporarily modified (in other words "visually messed up"), you can usually restore integrity to the screen by first maximizing, then minimizing a screen window.

Another point to consider when you run a Magic Trick program is that some of them consume considerable time and resources. For example, the algorithms for generating complex fractal graphics take a lot of CPU time. If you are running any other Windows programs at the same time as a Magic Trick program, it may be affected. You can adversely impact the performance of other programs.

Try out the programs on a system that does not have a lot of other activity. In fact, the more complex your hardware setup, or the busier your multitasking software environment, the more likely you will be to run into potential conflicts.

Of course, that is always the case when you run multiple programs under Windows. Exercise some restraint when you try out a group of new programs. Don't try to run sixty new programs all at once. Nearly all computer programs have bugs in them somewhere. A program may fail on one computer system, yet work perfectly on the next. A program may even work today on your system, but not work tomorrow when you happen to be running something else with which the new program conflicts.

The programs in this book have all been tested on 386 computers using different amounts of memory, different clock speeds, and different video cards. I have tried the programs using standard VGA as well as Super VGA. Perhaps even more importantly, all programs work under both Windows 3.0 and 3.1 in our test systems. Of course, that does not necessarily mean that all programs will always work on all unknown combinations of CPU, memory, video cards, and additional hardware boards. If a Magic Trick program does not work for you, try to simplify your executing environment by closing some windows or other applications.

♠ ♥ ♦ ♣

PART......

smoke & mirrors

How does the program do that? You'll be shaking your head in bewilderment when you see ants crawl around your screen, and eyes that wink, blink, and seem to follow the mouse around. I won't give away the authors' magical techniques. But you'll get to enjoy a wide range of unique effects.

Watch in amazement as bullet holes appear in your screen, miniaturized movies appear and horses gallop in icons, fish swim across your screen, and even submarines and mermaids occasionally appear while you work.

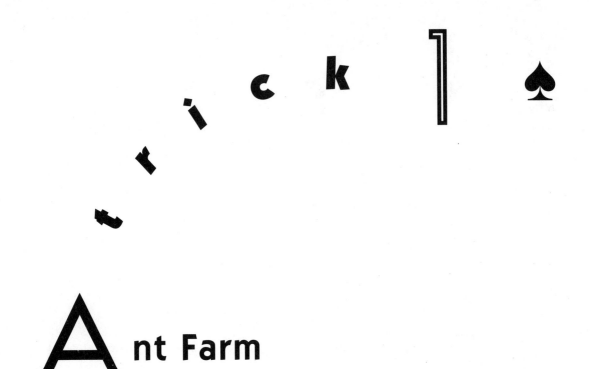

Ant Farm

.the big picture

Tim Hoffman whipped up this Ant Farm (ANTS.EXE) program as the first in a series of animated backgrounds for Windows. The program produces a colony of ants that crawl around the desktop. Don't worry, they won't interfere with the other work you may be doing. The ants crawl behind all open windows and icons on your screen.

.running the program

Once you've activated the program, the ants crawl at random across the desktop. They won't crawl beyond the screen boundary, and each

■ The ants go marching, one by one.

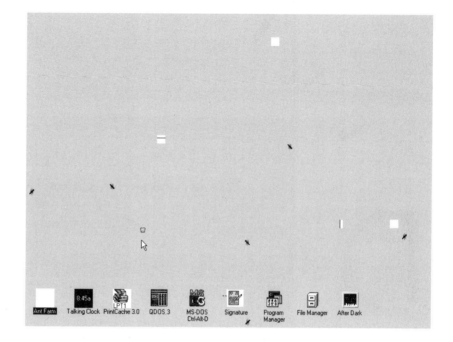

ant will run away from the other ants it encounters—until the slice of bread appears. The ants are magically attracted to the slice of bread. Tim says that the bread looks crude, since he only spent three minutes with a bitmap editor to create it. Actually, the slice of bread looks kind of cute.

■ ■ ■ ■ ■ ■ ■ ■ ■ ■ ■ ■ ■ ■ ■ ■ **behind the trick**

If you have any suggestions for Tim Hoffman regarding his free-ware program, you can bug him in the following ways:

> BBS: Llama Bob's BBS at (214) 890-0BOB (HST 14.4k)
> FidoNet echo: The WINDOWS.PROG echo
> NetMail: 1:124/6003

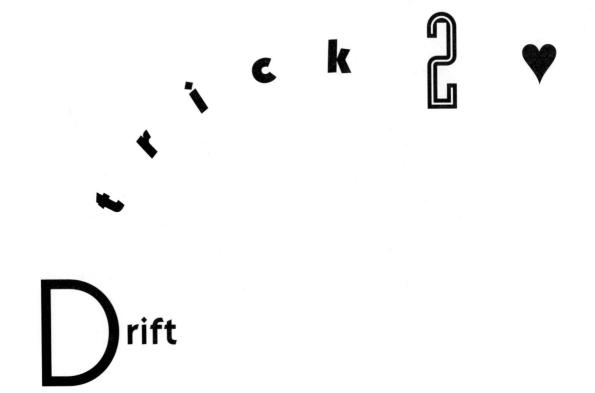

trick 2 ♥

Drift

●the big picture

The Drift (DRIFT.EXE) program makes all the windows and icons on your desktop meander across the screen. You are hereby cautioned against the possible physical damage that may be done to your person if you run this program on someone else's computer. The program has no damaging effects to your disk or your data, but the visual havoc it causes can be distracting at the very least and distressing at the very most.

■ Do you
sometimes have
trouble keeping
track of things?

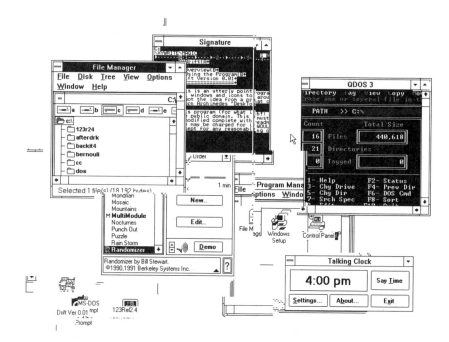

• • • • • • • • • • • • running the program

Just run the Drift program. As long as it is active and its icon
remains on the screen, the icons and windows on your screen will
wander around the desktop. Soon you'll have a lot of trouble determining exactly where an icon or window is. The windows and
icons leave trails that overlap the actual positions of windows or
icons. Soon you will will have no idea where to find each window's
Control menu.

Pay attention to where the Drift icon is. You want to be able to close
the program when you've had enough. If you can't locate the Drift
icon, remember that you can always press Ctrl-Esc to display the
Task Manager. From the Task Manager dialog box, highlight DRIFT
and press the End Task button to stop the icons from drifting.

■ ■ ■ ■ ■ ■ ■ ■ ■ ■ ■ ■ ■ ■ ■ ■ **behind the trick**

The author of Drift is Nick Waltham. He got the idea for it from a progam that came with the Acorn Archimedes "DeskTop." He donates the program (for what its worth, he says) to the public domain. However, the program must be distributed unmodified and complete with the two files found in your SYBEX\DRIFT directory. No fee may be charged for the program except for reasonable copying charges.

Naturally, Nick accepts no responsibility (who does?) for loss or damage incurred as a result of this freeware program. Nevertheless, the program is not a virus and has no damaging consequences. It's just sort of cute and makes you wonder how it works.

Address any comments to Nick at

e-mail: SPEEDY@UK.AC.OX.VAX

Nick is simply interested in seeing see how far his program travels!

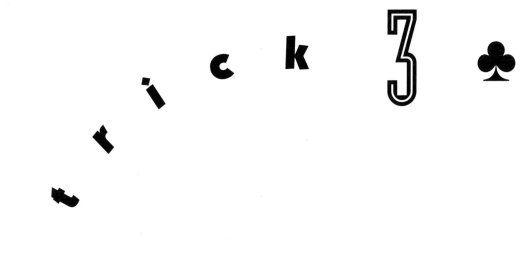

Eyecon

■ ■ ■ ■ ■ ■ ■ ■ ■ ■ ■ ■ ■ ■ ■ ■ ■ ■ **the big picture**

The Eyecon (EYECON.EXE) program implements a popular UNIX workstation program called "xeyes." It features an icon with a pair of eyes that follow the mouse cursor wherever it goes.

■ Ever have the feeling that you're being watched?

▪ ▪ ▪ ▪ ▪ ▪ ▪ ▪ ▪ ▪ ▪ ▪ ▪ ▪ ▪running the program

Just run the program and the icon eye appears. You can drag the icon anywhere on the screen you like, and it will keep looking back at you. If you don't move the mouse for 60 seconds, one of the eyes shuts—that is, it falls asleep. After another 60 seconds, both eyes shut. As soon as you move the mouse, the icon wakes up and opens its eyes again.

If you like the falling asleep aspect of the icon, you can adjust the sleep interval. To do so, add two lines to your WIN.INI file:

```
[EyeCon]
Timer=25
```

The Timer variable specifies the interval, in seconds, between the time you stop moving your mouse and the time the first eye shuts. For example, setting the Timer to a value of 25 makes one eye shut after 25 seconds of inactivity on the part of the mouse. After another 25 seconds of inactivity, both eyes shut.

▪ ▪ ▪ ▪ ▪ ▪ ▪ ▪ ▪ ▪ ▪ ▪ ▪ ▪ ▪ behind the trick

EyeCon is a proprietary freeware program written by Nobuya Higashiyama. You may contact him at

Nobuya Higashiyama
642-D Residenz Parkway
Kettering, OH 45429
(513) 293-9320
CompuServe: 71570,533
Internet: nxh@meaddata.com
UUCP: …!uunet!meaddata!nxh

Eyes

the big picture

■ ■ ■ ■ ■ ■ ■ ■ ■ ■ ■ ■ ■ ■ ■ ■

The Eyes (EYES.EXE) program displays a set of eyes on the desktop that move along with your cursor across the screen. The eyes also have a number of other small features. They can wink, blink, and nod. You can even name them yourself.

■ "Come quickly. I'm sure the computer just winked at me."

running the program

The Eyes program displays the icon with the winking, blinking, nodding eyeballs. When you drag the Eyes icon to a new position, it winks at you. The eyes icon also blinks at random—just like real eyes. How realistic!

If your mouse does not move for a period of time, the eyes fall asleep. When you begin to move the mouse pointer again, the eyes open again and follow the pointer as before.

behind the trick

Chris Eisnaugle claims credit for this cute little freeware program, and hopes that you enjoy it. Please send comments and suggestions to him at

CompuServe: 76166,1257

Fatbits

the big picture

The Fatbits (FATBITS.EXE) program is a pixel magnifier program for Windows. It magnifies the pixels in the area of the screen around the cursor and places the giant pixels in a small, tastefully decorated window.

running the program

Fatbits is one of those extraordinarily useful utility programs for people writing Windows software. If you're not a Windows programmer, it can still satisfy your intellectual curiosity by showing you exactly how screen images are constructed. This program

▫ Fatbits can show you the pixel makeup of any screen image.

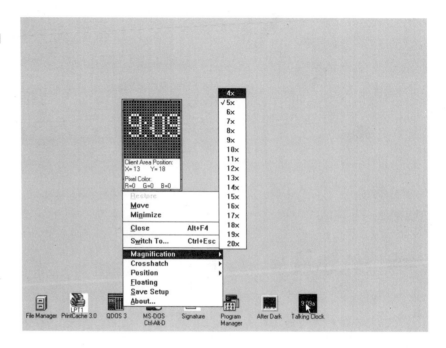

is indispensable if you want to see a screen image right down to the last pixel.

Fatbits is a reimplementation of a Macintosh desk accessory that's been around since the beginning. However, this program is a little more useful than its Mac predecessor because, with Windows multitasking, you can leave the Fatbits window open and continue to use other programs while it runs.

As the figure shows, several options are available with this program. Access any of them by clicking once in a Fatbits window to make Fatbits display its Control menu. The Control menu contains a number of useful options. Options with a right-pointing arrow by their side have their own secondary submenus.

For instance, the Magnification choice offers seventeen levels of magnification. To select one, just click once on the magnifying number you wish. All the Fatbits menus will close and the main Fatbits window will refocus itself instantly to the new magnification level. Depending on how detailed the screen image that you are studying is, the magnification feature can make it significantly easier to explore and determine its makeup and the color composition of its pixels.

The Crosshatch choice offers four subordinate choices: None, White, Black, and Invert. With these choices, you can control the pixel grid that appears in the Fatbits window.

The Position choice lets you know exactly which pixel on your screen is being magnified. You can ask for Absolute, Relative, or Client Area Positioning information. The absolute positioning numbers would range from a top-left corner value of (0,0) to a bottom-right screen corner value of (639,479) for a VGA screen, or (799,599) for a Super VGA screen.

Client area positioning can be very interesting and very revealing. As you can see in the figure, the mouse pointer is on the Talking Clock icon at the bottom of the screen. In the figure, Fatbits is displaying client area positioning, and the tip of the mouse pointer is located at an X value of 13 and a Y value of 18. The X value always goes from left to right and the Y value from top to bottom. The "window" used by an icon is always fixed at 32 bits square.

behind the trick

Fatbits was written by John Ridges. It is freeware, which John says means that you may use it without paying him so much as a penny. You can also give it to your friends and neighbors, or upload it to other BBS's as long as both files in the FATBITS directory stay together and are not modified.

If you have any comments, questions, suggestions (or even hate mail, John says), you can contact him at

CompuServe: 72000,2057 (checked weekly)

trick 6 ♥

Fish!

■ ■ ■ ■ ■ ■ ■ ■ ■ ■ ■ ■ ■ ■ ■ ■ ■ ■ **the big picture**

The Fish! (FISH.EXE) program combines an animated wallpaper feature with a colorful and animated screen-saver. Both features present a beautiful and creative array of sea life that swims around your desktop.

■ ■ ■ ■ ■ ■ ■ ■ ■ ■ ■ ■ ■ ■ ■ **running the program**

The Fish! program includes its own graphic editor for creating, editing, and defining the movements of new fish. As you'll discover, fish aren't the only things that swim in this aquarium. Scuba divers, mermaids and mermen, and moving bubbles that float to

■ Enjoy this carefree, diversely populated aquarium.

File Manager PrintCache 3.0 QDOS 3 MS-DOS Signature Program After Dark Talking Clock
Ctrl-Alt-D Manager

Fish! 3.0a4, Copyright 1990, Tom and Ed's Bogus Software, All Rights Reserved

the surface can be found there too. You can be completely creative, both in how you define your own personalized aquarium and what you place inside it.

When you first run the Fish! program, the background wallpaper on your Windows desktop turns instantly into a colorful, imaginative, and entertaining aquarium. Bubbles of air float to the surface, and a variety of beautifully designed fish swim up, down, and around.

By clicking anywhere on the wallpaper, you can display the Fish! System menu. It consists of five choices: Edit Fish, Screen Saver, Preferences, About, and Exit.

■ ■ ■ ■ ■ ■ ■ ■ ■ ■ ■ ■ ■ ■ **customizing the fish**

Use the Fish Editor to customize fish species or to create a species of your own. First, select Edit Fish to display the Fish Editor dialog box, which is shown in the figure.

■ Create new species of fish.

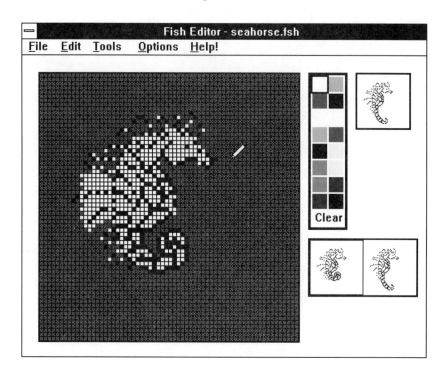

With the Fish Editor, you can discover complete details about all the fish files included in this package.

Look at an existing fish file by choosing Open from the File menu. Fish files have the extension .FSH. Choose the fish file you want from the list of files shown, or type in the path name of the file you want. You can save your changes by choosing Save from the File menu, or you can save your current work to a new file by choosing Save As.

Go ahead and experiment with your own designs. You can create your favorite fish, perhaps a Japanese koi, or create some other frivolity such as a submarine. Pull down the various menus in the Fish Editor to see what you can do. The Edit menu allows you to do conventional cut, copy, paste, and clear operations, which means you can even use graphic images that you've created or captured elsewhere.

The Tools menu offers three choices: Draw, Select, and Fill. The default tool is the one that you can see in the Figure above—a drawing pen. The drawing pen deposits a single pixel of color whenever you click the mouse. Choose a color by clicking on the color chart on the right side of the Fish Editor window.

The Select tool lets you mark off and work with a rectangular portion of the editing area. Use Select with the principal Edit commands, such as Copy, Cut, and Paste. You can use the Fill tool to apply color to a closed area within the overall editing area. The Fill tool changes the mouse pointer to an image of a gasoline pump. To deposit the currently chosen color into all pixels within a closed path, move the pump to a pixel within the selected area and click once. If you do not click inside a closed area, the Editor will colorize all pixels that lie outside closed areas.

The Options menu offers three options: Motion, Enabled, and Rare. Click on Enabled if you want your fish design to appear at some time, either on the wallpaper or on the screen-saver. The fish will appear frequently or infrequently, depending on whether you've clicked on the Rare choice. Both Enabled and Rare are toggle switches. When you click on Motion, the Fish Motion dialog box appears. Here you specify how your fish will move. The choices are easy to understand on this dialog box.

the screen-saver

Normally, the Fish! program treats you to its images as part of your Windows wallpaper, and the fish swim behind open windows and icons. However, you can configure Fish! to activate itself as a screen-saver. In that case, the windows and icons are temporarily erased and the fish swim across the entire screen until you either press a key or move the mouse again.

To activate Screen-Saver mode, click on the desktop to select Screen Saver from the main System menu. The Screen Saver Options dialog box appears. Type a number into the Sleep After field to represent the number of minutes you want the program to be dormant before the screen-saver kicks in. If your system shows no mouse or keyboard activity during this time, you'll see the screen-saver.

behind the trick

The version of Fish! in this book is the pre-release version of Fish 3.0. To become a registered user and receive the latest version of this shareware program, send $24.95 to

Tom & Ed's Bogus Software
15600 NE Eighth Street
Suite A3334
Bellevue, WA 98008

Yes, Ted & Ed's Bogus Software is a real name. You can thank Ed Fries and Tom Saxton for this highly entertaining piece of work. You can also thank Kathy Conley and her friends for the artwork evident in the design of the seagoing denizens.

the big picture

This collection of Fun programs draws faces, eyes, screen cracks, and various bugs at random on the desktop. It does this at random intervals once you initiate one or more of the programs.

running the program

Seven individual programs come with this collection. Each one does its own thing, and you can run any one or several of the programs in the usual way. To make the figure, I initiated several programs at once. Notice that, except for EYES.EXE, no icons appear on your desktop, nor do any entries appear in the Task Manager

▫ Who ya gonna call?—Screen busters!

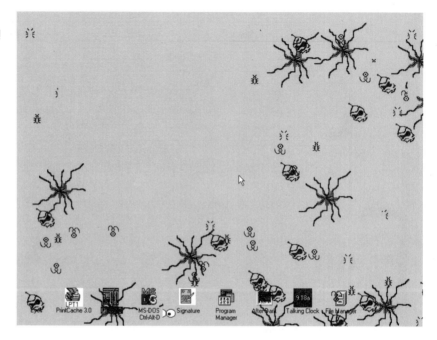

list. However, although the programs don't have icons, each expires by itself and either exits automatically or asks you if you wish it to exit.

FACE.EXE draws 100 faces at random on the screen, at random intervals. Then it asks the user if he or she has had enough. If the user clicks Yes, the program stops drawing the faces and exits Windows.

BURST.EXE is similar to FACE except that it waits one full minute before doing anything. Then it begins painting small cracks on the screen. Each time a crack appears, the user hears a cracking sound.

BURST2.EXE waits a random amount of time (no less than 1 minute) before painting a very large cracked area in the center of the screen. Then it exits.

WIZ.EXE is similar to FACE.EXE, except that this face is that of the robot from the movie "Wizards."

EYES.EXE draws a pair of eyes on the screen that follow the mouse cursor. Every once in a while, the eyes move randomly to another part of the screen.

BUGS.EXE draws four types of bugs on the screen for a random time period and then exits.

FRIED.EXE is a program that only activates on a Friday the 13th. On that day, it puts up a message that says

" **Help me I'm a bug!!! **"**

Then it automatically runs BUGS.EXE and exits.

behind the trick

Be careful if you use this or any of the other programs—except EYES.EXE—in this package on someone else's computer. The programs eventually stop running, but the unsuspecting person will never know it. It's easy to panic about viruses and the like. Someone might reboot the system too quickly and perhaps lose some real work in the process.

You can register the Fun programs for $10.00 a piece by contacting their author:

Michael Harrison
Dragon's Eye Software
P.O. Box 200262
Arlington, TX 76006-0262
817-265-5619 (orders and customer service)
800-242-4775 (credit card orders only)
CompuServe: 76057,101

Gatling Gun

■ **.the big picture**

The Gatling (GATLING.EXE) program periodically sprays bullets across your computer screen, leaving a trail of bullet holes in your windows. The bullet holes remain on-screen until Windows itself brings up new windows.

■ ■ ■ ■ ■ ■ ■ ■ ■ ■ ■ ■ ■ ■ **.running the program**

The Gatling program normally displays an icon with a bullet hole in it. By default, the program sprays a random series of bullet holes across your screen every once in a while. If you're going to be in-sidious and run this program on someone else's computer, you can

■ When good
computers go bad.

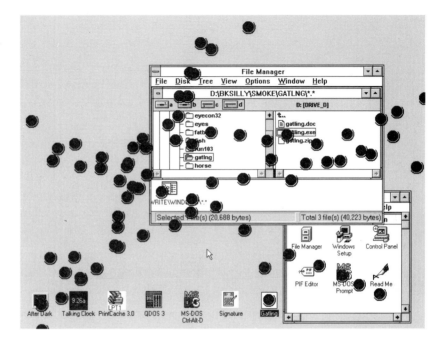

control several execution settings. For instance, you can control the average time interval between gun bursts. In fact, you can even hide the existence of the program with another option. All optional settings are found on the icon's Control Menu. To display all choices, just click once on the Gatling icon.

The author suggests some uses for his program. He says that if you have a tendency to fall asleep in front of your keyboard during long word-processing sessions, or if you often fall asleep late at night while playing games, you could use Gatling—with the sound turned on—to wake yourself up every so often.

The program's normal mode is to blast the screen at time intervals of about 90 seconds on average, with a minimum time of 30 seconds between blasts. You can modify this operation with a command line parameter specifying a new average interval in seconds. The minimum interval used will be one fifth of the average interval value. Each blast can take 2 seconds or more, so an average value of less than 10 seconds is not recommended!

This version of Gatling also supports several System menu options. The Refresh option removes all trace of battle damage by repainting the background of the desktop and all the application windows or icons.

The Hide Gatling option hides the program's application icon, which, as mentioned above, has the side-effect of removing the program from the task list. With the icon hidden, you have to exit Windows if you want to stop Gatling from executing. In other words, don't leave the program running unattended on someone else's machine because they won't know how to stop it.

The Timer Interval option brings up a dialog box for changing the average time interval between machine gun blasts. The current timer interval setting is also shown in the option's menu string.

The Sound Effects option is a switch that lets you turn off the sometimes annoying machine gun sound effects.

The Small, Medium, and Large Caliber options, taken as a group, are for changing the size of the bullet holes on the screen. All sizes work on all monitors, but often one size looks better than the others due to differences in screen resolution.

▪ ▪ ▪ ▪ ▪ ▪ ▪ ▪ ▪ ▪ ▪ ▪ ▪ ▪ ▪ ▪ behind the trick

Gatling is Scott Gourley's copyrighted Machine Gun Screen Blaster program for Microsoft Windows. You can contact him at

> Clickon Software
> 105 Union Street
> Watertown, MA 02172
> (617) 924-5761
> CompuServe: 72311,613

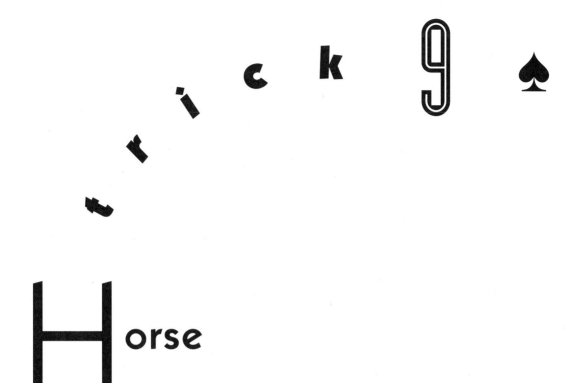

trick 9 ♠

Horse

The Horse (HORSE.EXE) program draws a picture of a galloping horse in a small window. You can leave it running without putting a strain on your system and use it as a desktop decoration. However, you can't resize the Horse window. If you minimize the window, a slightly truncated version of the galloping horse appears in the icon-size box.

▪ Hi-Ho
Silver…Away!

▪ ▪ ▪ ▪ ▪ ▪ ▪ ▪ ▪ ▪ ▪ ▪ ▪ ▪ ▪ running the program

Run Horse any way you like to bring up the galloping horse's window. It is intended to be used as a desktop decoration and to be initiated when you start Windows.

Here's a cute trick to try. Start up sixteen copies of Horse. After you've admired the stampede on your screen for a few seconds, start closing the windows, starting with the first one and leaving the sixteenth for last. As each window is closed, the horse in the sixteenth window will gallop faster and faster.

▪ ▪ ▪ ▪ ▪ ▪ ▪ ▪ ▪ ▪ ▪ ▪ ▪ ▪ ▪ ▪ ▪ behind the trick

James M. Curran lies behind this program, but asks no registration fee for it. He writes to me that his goal is to make Horse a standard part of every Windows desktop in America. Sort of like Microsoft wanting to make Windows a standard part of every desktop in America. Good luck, James.

James offers this copyrighted program free to the public in the hope of making everyone's computer a nicer place to visit. You can contact him at

James M. Curran
24 Greendale Road
Cedar Grove, NJ 07009-1313
CompuServe: 72261,655

Icon Frightener

the big picture

Ever wonder what would happen if your application icons suddenly got frightened of the mouse cursor? Or if you tried to click on an application to open it, and the icon ran away? Well, now you can afflict your icons with "cursorphobia" by running the Icon Frightener (ICOFRITE.EXE) for Windows!

running the program

Run Icon Frightener any way you like. Be aware, however, that to end the program you have to bring up the Task Manager either by

◻ An exercise-in-futility utility: Icons that run away from the mouse pointer.

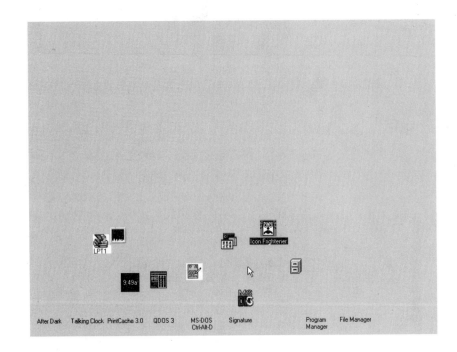

double-clicking on the desktop background or by pressing Ctrl-Esc. Next, highlight ICOFRITE and click on the End Task button. You can also bring up Icofrite's System menu by pressing Alt-spacebar and selecting Close.

If you decide to secretly load this program on your friends' machines, just be sure they don't have a history of heart trouble, and don't let them wear out their mouse trying to click on the icons before you tell them what's going on. This program is harmless to the Windows environment and to PC files, but it can cause grave harm to your friends' dispositions!

If you touch the frame of an open application window with the cursor, Icofrite will turn the window into an icon. It will be just as scared of the cursor as all your other desktop icons are!

If you press Alt-spacebar to bring up Icofrite's system menu, you will discover some additional choices:

- **Refresh** lines up all the scattered icons on a neatly ordered row at the bottom of the screen. You will wonder if electric shock therapy was used to accomplish this, but Icofrite likes to keep its treatment methods confidential.

- **About** displays a dialog box with author and version information.

- **Hide IcoFrite** hides the program's application icon, which has the effect of removing the program from the task list as well. With the icon hidden, you have to exit Windows to stop IcoFrite from executing. In other words, you probably shouldn't leave this program running unattended with a hidden icon on someone else's machine!

behind the trick

Icofrite is Scott Gourley's copyrighted Icon Frightener program for Microsoft Windows. Scott is also the author of Gatling, which may be found elsewhere in this book. You can contact him at

Clickon Software
105 Union Street
Watertown, MA 02172
(617) 924-5761
CompuServe: 72311,613

This program is freeware, but if you would like to see more programs of this type from Scott (he says he has ideas for twenty more programs like this), feel free to send him a donation. If he gets a good response, he says he will consider putting together a collection called the "Windows Un-productivity Pack."

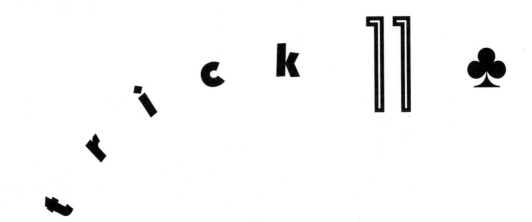

trick 11 ♣

Icon Movies

● ● ● ● ● ● ● ● ● ● ● ● ● ● ● ● ● ● **.the big picture**

Here is the pre-multimedia version of movies on your desktop. Each movie is shown inside its own icon.

▪ Windows goes to the movies; you provide the popcorn.

running the program

James Bell has produced what he admits are the world's silliest Windows programs! Naturally, in the context of this book, he may have an argument about whether his programs deserve that particular accolade.

Three tiny movies are included in this package. You can run each of them separately by simply initiating the appropriate executable program.

BALL.EXE shows a bouncing ball that appears to be subject to no known force of physics, including gravity. It will bounce and bounce and bounce and bounce.

BOXING.EXE gives you an opportunity to watch the Friday Night Fights without anyone actually getting bruised or bloodied. The movie is more like a Batman comic strip, complete with Pow! and Bam! effects. The winning boxer jumps for joy before embarking on his next fight immediately.

AIR.EXE demonstrates the mini-animation art of paper airplane folding to the ultimate degree. Watch your paper airplane go down the runway and take off for a brief flight.

behind the trick

James Bell is responsible for these cute little shareware movie icons. To register your copy of Icon Movies with him and receive the latest version of the programs (he may have developed other mini-movie icons), send $5.00 to

James Bell
4511 Sherwood Trace
Gainesville, FL 32605
(904) 372-3695

Lens

The Lens (LENS.EXE) program by Ned Konz magnifies the area of the screen around the mouse cursor. The magnified graphics appear in the Lens window, as you can see in the figure.

Lens is a Windows version of an Amiga program Ned wrote several years ago. The Windows version runs faster than the earlier Amiga version, probably because it uses a special Windows function call, the StretchBlt( ) function.

■ A personalized zoom lens to show greater detail.

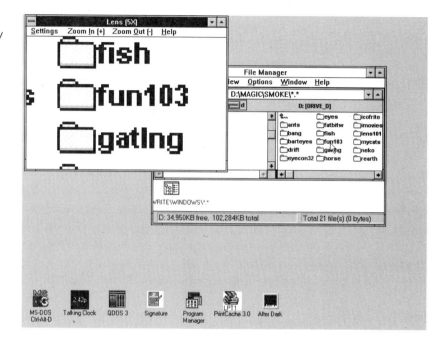

When you run Lens, the area around the mouse pointer appears magnified in the Lens window. In the figure, the mouse pointer is in the File Manager window, and the Lens window shows a five-fold magnification of the small area around the mouse. Notice the "5x" in the title bar.

Besides tracking the mouse cursor, Lens can track the caret—that is, the "text cursor" in text applications. To track the text cursor, enable Track Caret mode by checking its toggle switch on the Settings menu. A dialog box appears asking you to confirm your request: You can enable Track Caret mode and track the text cursor in Notepad or any other Windows or non-Windows application that runs in Text mode. However, Lens will not work with all applications. It will not work, for instance, with Word for Windows or with other applications that use built-in Windows calls for displaying and moving the caret. Because Lens can't tell whether a caret is actually being displayed, toggling to Track Caret mode may keep Lens from following the mouse when a non-text program is active. The Lens program tracks the mouse cursor when the caret is in the upper-left corner (0,0) of the active window; otherwise it tracks the caret.

By activating Repeat mode, you can magnify the contents of a window as it changes no matter whether the mouse or the caret is being moved. For example, with Repeat mode, you could magnify any program in this book that uses animation or varying graphics output. However, Repeat mode can be a resource hog and slow down your system if the timerInterval setting is too short. For this reason, Lens asks you to confirm that you want and understand what happens in Repeat mode.

You can enlarge or reduce magnification by clicking on the Zoom In (+) or the Zoom Out (−) menu choices. Alternatively, you can more rapidly zoom in or out faster by pressing the gray plus or minus key. Magnification ranges from 1X (normal size) to 20X (a twenty-fold magnification).

You can display or hide the Lens menu bar. By hiding the menu bar, you enlarge the window area within which Lens can present magnified images. Menu bar choices are also available on the application's System menu, so you can always control Lens by opening up the System menu. In fact, you'll have to do this if you want to redisplay the menu bar.

▪ ▪ ▪ ▪ ▪ ▪ ▪ ▪ ▪ ▪ ▪ ▪ ▪ ▪ ▪ ▪ behind the trick

Lens was written and copyrighted by Ned Konz. If his freeware program has value to you, he'd really appreciate some kind of payment—such as five dollar bills, source code, good beer, etc. You may contact him at

Ned Konz
161 14th Street
Holly Hill, FL 32117

Neko

the big picture

This program is another example of fun animation. The cat—Neko means "cat" in Japanese—is attracted to the mouse pointer and runs towards it. Unfortunately for the cat, it can only catch the mouse if the mouse is inside the Neko window.

running the program

Run the Neko (NEKO.EXE) program and the window in the figure appears. The cat in the window will begin to run toward your mouse pointer, wherever it is on the screen. Indoor mice can usually find safety on the other side of your walls, as can the mouse pointer on

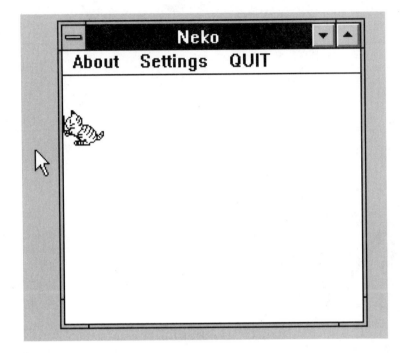

□ Neko is an indoors cat. This mouse can get away to play another day.

your screen. As long as the mouse pointer stays outside the walls of the Neko box, it is safe from the cat. The cat can't get out and catch the mouse. He can only scratch at the wall, as seen in the figure, and dream of better days.

But if the cat catches the mouse inside the Neko box, it's a different story. Soon, however, just like a real cat, Neko realizes that catching the prey takes all the fun out of the chase. The cat sits there for a moment trying to figure out what to do next. Then it scratches itself and curls up for a nap. Try moving the mouse pointer again and the cat will wake up and start the chase again.

Click on the Settings menu choice to display the Neko Settings dialog box. The three choices here let you influence this interesting cat-and-mouse game.

You can set the time in milliseconds for how often Neko is drawn on the screen while it chases the mouse. The larger the value you set for this Time variable, the smoother your cat is going to move.

The Speed variable controls the number of pixels that Neko leaps each time it is redrawn. The smaller the number you enter for Travel Distance, the smaller the steps the cat takes when it runs. If you enter a small number, the cat is going to have a hard time catching the mouse. On the other hand, entering a very large number here creates an effect similar to a transportation beam in a science fiction movie: the cat appears almost instantaneously beside the mouse, no matter how far or fast you try to move the mouse pointer.

Finally, the Idle option lets you specify how sensitive your cat will be to the movements of the mouse. The smaller you make this number, the less distance the mouse has to move on-screen before being noticed by the cat. The cat will leap up and run toward the mouse whenever you move the mouse pointer the number of pixels you enter under the Idle option.

▪ ▪ ▪ ▪ ▪ ▪ ▪ ▪ ▪ ▪ ▪ ▪ ▪ ▪ ▪ ▪ ▪behind the trick

This lively little magic trick was written originally by Masayuki Koba, but this version has been done by Dara T. Khani. You may freely copy it, as long as you distribute it without modification. You can reach the author at

Dara T. Khani
1088 McKinnon Ave.
Oviedo, FL 32765
Internet: darak@iplmail.orl.mmc.com

Rotating Earth

■ ■ ■ ■ ■ ■ ■ ■ ■ ■ ■ ■ ■ ■ ■ ■ **the big picture**

The Rotating Earth (REARTH.EXE) program displays an icon with a miniaturized rotating globe.

■ Get an astronaut's view of the planet earth.

running the program

The earth will move for you when you run this program. It may not be as good as making the earth move under your feet, but it's the best that this program can do.

If you want to get really fancy, try running Rotating Earth multiple times. You can actually run it up to thirty times before a message appears to tell you that there are now too many timers. Why would you want to do this? At the very least, you could try to simulate the twenty-four time zones. In any case, having thirty globes spinning separately presents a revolutionary view of our planet.

behind the trick

This program is freeware, so there is no registration information and no fees are charged. You can do what you want with the executable module. The best I can do here is credit Andy Galassi as the author, according to information I found in the .EXE file.

System Usage Thermometers

■ .the big picture

The System Usage Thermometers (SYSUSE.EXE) program presents red thermometer gauges, or an alternative digital display, to show the current utilization levels of your computer's four main resources: CPU, memory, system resources, and disk space.

■ These thermometers can measure more than flu and cold symptoms.

SysUse

▭	SysUse	▼
	CPU: 76%	
	Memory: 11%	
	Resources: 23%	
	Disk: 83%	

▫ ▫ ▫ ▫ ▫ ▫ ▫ ▫ ▫ ▫ ▫ ▫ running the program

When you first run this program, you see a digital display like the one on the right side of the figure. I ran the program twice to show you, side by side, the two display possibilities. However, the thermometer display is actually the program's dynamic icon. Even if you don't configure SysUse to display the thermometer group and you display the digital presentation instead, you will see the gauges when you minimize the normal SysUse display.

Perhaps you use a number of applications on your system and you're tired of seeing two, three, or even four icons at the bottom of your screen monitoring the different aspects of your computer. If this is the case, SysUse is for you. In one small window, and even in one small icon, you can monitor the performance of your Windows system.

SysUse is very efficient, especially when it's minimized, and takes very little time away from your other applications. SysUse was intended to be launched from the WIN.INI file. In fact, in order to get accurate readings for the CPU and memory, you must load it before you load other applications. This is because CPU speed and total available memory are initialized when SysUse first comes up. Be sure to give SysUse a minute or so to adjust to your CPU's speed.

You will discover two unique commands on SysUse's System menu: About SysUse and Options. About SysUse displays the usual program and author information. Options brings up a dialog box for setting the following program options:

- ▫ **Recalibrate CPU**—Causes the CPU speed to be reinitialized. Select this option if your CPU level appears to be incorrect. For example, if a CPU value or level is greater than 0 even though nothing else is running, you might consider the Recalibrate CPU option.

◻ **Compact Memory**—Calls the GlobalCompact Windows function to compact global memory. Select this option if Windows reports that memory is insufficient to run an application even though there appears to be enough memory. It may be that the free memory is just not contiguous.

◻ **Drives**—Selects one or more disk drives to be monitored. Be careful about selecting floppy drives, because they can be pretty slow.

◻ **Update**—Selects the update period for the SysUse window and icon. Usage levels may be recalculated and displayed every one, two, or three seconds. One second is the default.

◻ **OK**—Exits the Options dialog box.

When you close SysUse or exit Windows, the above options and the position of the SysUse window are saved to your WIN.INI file. These settings automatically take effect the next time you run SysUse.

◻ ◻ ◻ ◻ ◻ ◻ ◻ ◻ ◻ ◻ ◻ ◻ ◻ ◻ ◻ **behind the trick**

SysUse is a shareware program, so you are welcome to try it out free of charge. However, if you like it and decide to keep it on your system, you are obligated to register your copy by paying $5.95 to the author at the address given below. Registration entitles you to legal use of this and all future releases of SysUse, notification of future releases, and technical support.

As with so many other shareware programs, the SysUse author wants to point out that this program is provided as-is, without warranty of any kind, either express or implied. No liability is assumed from any damage or loss resulting from the use of this program.

You are free to copy and share SysUse with others, as long as the SYSUSE11.EXE and SYSUSE11.TXT files are distributed together and not modified in any way. Shareware distributors are permitted to include SysUse with their distributions, but any fee charged by the distributor does not cover the $5.95 registration fee. This is the amount that users owe to the author if they decide to keep and use SysUse. Businesses, government agencies, and other organizations may purchase a site license by contacting the author for additional information.

To register your copy of SysUse, send a check or money order for $5.95 to

Jonathan Reed
1575 Agnes Avenue
Palm Bay, FL 32909
CompuServe: 70570,3171
Prodigy: rdts35a

t r i c k 16 ◆

TopCAT!

■ ■ ■ ■ ■ ■ ■ ■ ■ ■ ■ ■ ■ ■ ■ ■ ■ **.the big picture**

The TopCAT! (TOPCAT.EXE) program draws a cat on your screen that chases your mouse pointer everywhere.

■ Mice beware! Neither windows nor icons will stay this cat from catching its prey.

running the program

Just like a real cat, this cat realizes that catching the prey takes all the fun out of the chase. The cat sits there for a moment trying to figure out what to do next. Then it scratches itself and curls up for a nap. When you move the mouse pointer again, the cat wakes up and renews the chase.

Click on the TopCAT! icon to display its System menu. Other than the standard Windows choices, only two choices are unique to this program, Freeze and Options.

Freeze instantly stops the cat's motion, regardless of where it is on the screen.

Options displays two additional choices for controlling your cat. The Update Frequency specifies how often you want the program to redraw the cat during the chase. The Travel Distance controls how many pixels the cat can leap each time it is redrawn. The smaller the number you enter for Travel Distance, the smaller the steps the cat takes when it runs. If you enter a small number, the cat is going to have a hard time catching the mouse. On the other hand, if you enter a larger number in the Update Frequency, the mouse is unlikely to avoid the cat.

behind the trick

Robert Dannbauer wrote this program. TopCAT! is very entertaining, owing to the fact that the cat can run right over windows and icons. The only information I have been able to discover about Robert is the following e-mail contact:

e-mail: robert@ruble.fml.tuwien.ac.at

♠ ♥ ♦ ♣

PART......

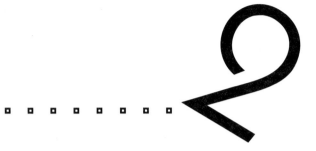

presto-change-o

Some programs can perform useful chores *and* do their work in interesting and entertaining ways. In this section you'll find a bevy of applications that provide valuable Windows functionality in engaging ways. Most of these programs offer single-shot capability. Run the program, click on an icon, or make a menu choice—a valuable and helpful system change instantly takes effect.

For example, double-click on a dolphin icon and watch the dolphin leap when your printer switches to portrait mode, or swim when it changes to landscape mode. Pop up a calendar window, or click on a keyhole icon to lock up your system with a password. Replace the traditional arrow pointer with something more entertaining, like a rocket or a long-tailed mouse. Add sound effects to your key presses, and control the loudness and pitch as well.

trick 17 ♠

Bang

......the big picture

The Bang (BANG.EXE) program enables you to fire a gun and shoot bullets anywhere on your screen. The program temporarily redefines the left mouse button so you can wield the mouse like a gun. Bang protects your hardware from physical abuse: when you've reached the point of frustration with an application, or even with Windows, it lets you vent your anger.

......running the program

When you run the Bang program, a mean-looking icon that looks like a holstered gun appears on your desktop. To draw and fire the

■ Don't get mad, get even with errant programs.

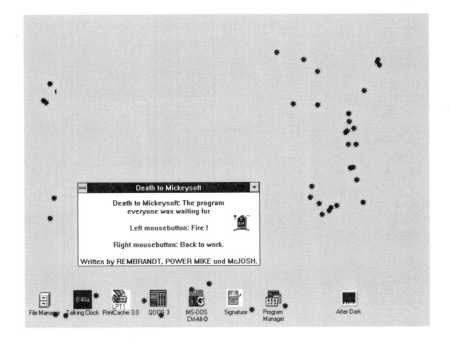

gun, you must restore the icon to full size. Do this by double-clicking on the icon. The window shown in the figure will appear on your screen. Now the mouse button redefinition logic is activated.

You can use the left mouse button to relieve your frustrations. Move the mouse itself to aim the gun, and press the left mouse button to fire it. Bullet holes appear in the screen where you point the mouse.

Press the right mouse button to return to normal Windows mode and to deactivate, or reholster, this special and unique weapon.

behind the trick

Bang is copyrighted by the Sirius Sybernetics Corporation. It was written by Heiner Eichmann, Michael Schuschk, and Jürgen Christ. This program is absolutely free. You can copy and use it freely. If you like this program, or just want to communicate with the authors, send them messages at

Z-Net: H.EICHMANN@OLN.ZER[.DE]
Internet: SCHUSCHK@C3PO.TNT.UNI-
HANNOVER.DBP.DE
Maus-Net: JUERGEN CHRIST@AC2.MAUS.DE

t r i c k 18 ♥

Big Cursor

Do you sometimes have trouble finding the mouse pointer? Is your screen so crowded with application windows that the mouse pointer occasionally gets lost? Perhaps you have a laptop with an LCD screen that doesn't display the mouse pointer as well as you'd like. The Big Cursor (BCURSOR.EXE) program solves these problems by doubling the size of the mouse pointer.

■ "The better to see you with, my dear."

running the program

Just run Big Cursor and your mouse pointer grows to twice its normal size. As long as you keep the Big Cursor icon on the screen, the mouse pointer remains doubled in size. To restore the mouse pointer to its original size, just close the Big Cursor application.

behind the trick

Not much is hiding behind this solitary executable file. James F. Cuddy gets credit for writing it because his name appears in the .EXE file. Big Cursor is a freeware program. If you know more about James, what else he's done, or how readers can contact him, please get in touch with me through the publisher of this book.

Calpop

♣

the big picture

Calpop (CALPOP.EXE) is a small program that displays any single month between January 1980 and December 2037. It's easy to switch from month to month or year to year quickly.

running the program

Calpop is one of several applications included in the Barry Press Utilities package. After you've completed the installation procedure, you will find a small group of Barry's programs in the BPUTILS directory.

■ What will the
future bring?

```
┌─────────────────────────────────────┐
│ ▭            CalPop                  │
│        November  1992                │
│                                      │
│    S   M   T   W   T   F   S         │
│    1   2   3   4   5   6   7         │
│    8   9  10  11  12  13  14         │
│   15  16  17  18  19  20  21         │
│   22  23  24  25  26  27  28         │
│   29  30                             │
│                                      │
│                                      │
│ ◄ │    │   │                    │ ► │
└─────────────────────────────────────┘
```

When you first run Calpop, it displays the current month. Notice
the arrow buttons on the scroll bar at the bottom of the Calpop display. Click the left arrow to move back one month or the right
arrow to move forward one month. Click on the white space inside
the scroll bar to change the year of the display.

To adjust the year from its minimum 1980 value to its maximum 2037
value, drag the scroll box to the right or left. Clearly, the author of this
program expects Windows to have a long and useful life.

You can use Calpop with keyboard as well as mouse controls. The
← and → keys correspond to the arrow buttons. Use the PgUp and
PgDn keys to scroll the year of the display, and the Home and End
keys to go from the first possible year, 1980, to the last possible
one, 2037.

■ ■ ■ ■ ■ ■ ■ ■ ■ ■ ■ ■ ■ ■ ■ ■ **behind the trick**

The Calpop program is one of a larger set of programs called The
Barry Press Utilities. Three programs from the larger utility set are
included on the disk that comes with this book. You'll find them in

the BPUTILS directory. They are called The Barry Press Utilities for Microsoft Windows, Computer Options Edition.

The entire set of programs and documentation is copyright 1991–1992 by Barry Press, and is released as shareware. If you use any of these utilities beyond a two-week evaluation period, you must send $20.00 in cash, a check, or a money-order to Barry Press at the address listed below.

Registration licenses a specific user on as many machines as are used solely by that user, or licenses a specific machine (not network servers) for an unlimited number of users. You may copy this software, subject to the $20.00 registration fee for each user or machine, freely as long as the entire collection is distributed without modification. Please accompany your registration with the form found on the disk (in the README.WRI file) so Barry can contact you about updates.

Registration of this *Windows Magic Tricks* book edition entitles you to receive the complete set of the Barry Press Utilities, including programs for text file comparison, script-driven printer orientation control, and program launch buttons resident anywhere on the desktop.

If you are interested in programming, the source code for these utilities is also available. Registered users may, for an additional $75.00, purchase a complete copy of the source code and related files for the entire set of utilities. The source code was developed with the Microsoft 6.00a C compiler and Windows SDK.

Although it remains the copyrighted property of Barry Press, the source code may be included by purchasers in other, larger derivative programs which are distributed or sold as long as the copyrighted source code is itself neither given away nor sold, and as long as the notice that portions are copyrighted by Barry Press appears clearly in the product.

No warranties are expressed or implied for this software, including merchantability or suitability for a particular purpose. No responsibility will be assumed by the author for any loss or damage due to its use.

You may contact Barry at

Barry Press
4201 Empress Avenue
Encino, CA 91436-3504
CompuServe: 72467,2353

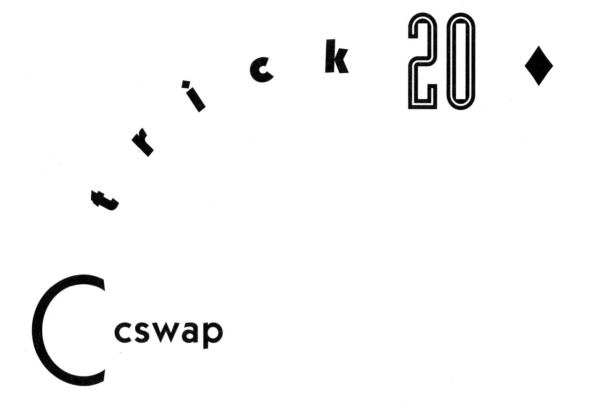

Ccswap

● ● ● ● ● ● ● ● ● ● ● ● ● ● ● ● ● **the big picture**

The Ccswap (CCSWAP.EXE) program performs a simple and sometimes helpful chore—it reverses the functionality of the Ctrl and the Caps Lock keys.

■ Lock into this
capital idea.

Ccswap

▪ ▪ ▪ ▪ ▪ ▪ ▪ ▪ ▪ ▪ ▪ ▪ ▪ ▪running the program

Simply run Ccswap and you'll see the icon shown here. As long as the icon remains on your screen, your Ctrl key will work like a Caps Lock key, and your Caps Lock key will work like a Ctrl key.

Fast typists who must frequently press Caps Lock to change the case of characters will like this program. It is easier to press Ctrl than Caps Lock because Ctrl is located at the lower-left corner of most keyboards. Once Ccswap has switched the keys' functionality, a quick dip of the left-hand pinky switches from upper- to lower-case and back again.

Ccswap only affects Windows programs. When you type text in a DOS program, the original key definitions apply, and the Ctrl and Caps Lock keys work in the usual way. There is an important issue to consider here. If you have defined Windows shortcut key combinations and they include the Ctrl key, the combinations will be affected even when you are using a DOS application.

▪ ▪ ▪ ▪ ▪ ▪ ▪ ▪ ▪ ▪ ▪ ▪ ▪ ▪ behind the trick

This novel—and quite limited in function—little freeware application was written for the public domain by David Michmerhuizen. You can reach him at

CompuServe: 70322,617

trick 21 ♠

Click

The Click (CLICK.EXE) program uses the PC's speaker to make a clicking sound whenever you press a key. You can change the duration and pitch of the click to adjust the sound and volume. Users who prefer the louder "click" you get from your system when you type under DOS will like this program.

running the program

Run the Click program and you'll see a computer key icon like the one in the figure. Click on this icon to display the Control menu, which offers the standard Windows choices as well as three unique

□ Create award-winning fingertip choreography.

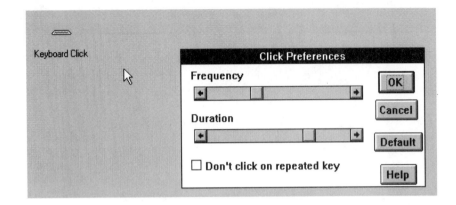

Click choices: Help, Preferences, and About.

- □ **Help** brings up a standard Help window with information about the Click program.

- □ **About** displays the author's name and contact information.

- □ **Preferences** displays the dialog box shown in the figure. From here you can control the frequency and duration of the clicking sound made when you press a key.

Move the slider boxes inside the scroll bars to the positions you like and click OK. If you want to keep the old settings, click Cancel. Each time you move a slider box, the Click program makes a sound so you can hear the frequency and duration settings you selected.

You may also choose to hear a "click" on repeated keys. A repeated key is one that continues to "click" when you press and hold it down. If you do not want to hear the clicking sound repeatedly, place an *X* in the check box labeled "Don't click on repeated key." Clear the box if you wish to hear repeated clicking sounds.

To restore Click's initial sound effects and return to the default frequency and duration, just click on the Default button in the Preferences dialog box.

Click will manage its sound effects only if you are using a Windows program. It will not work while you are typing in a DOS program.

behind the trick

David Feinleib has produced an interesting program here that provides certain users with just the kind of audible feedback they need. He would appreciate any comments, suggestions, or reports of problems. You can contact him at

> David A. Feinleib
> 1430 Massachusetts Avenue
> Suite 306-42
> Cambridge, MA 02138
> BIX: "pgm"
> CompuServe: 76516,20
> FidoNet: (IBM UG BBS, Boston MA.) David Feinleib

Click is shareware. You may make copies of this program and give them to others as long as the documentation is provided with the program, and both the documentation and program are not altered. If you like Click, a registration fee of $6.00 would be appreciated. You will receive support by mail, BIX, CompuServe, or FidoNet.

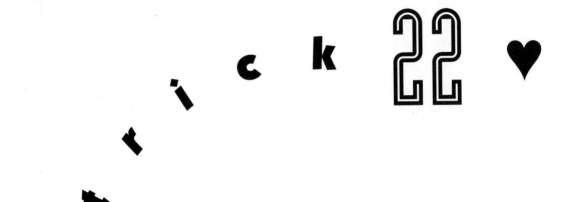

trick 22 ♥

Deus

■ ■ ■ ■ ■ ■ ■ ■ ■ ■ ■ ■ ■ ■**the big picture**

The Deus (DEUS.EXE) program offers a Macintosh-like visual alternative to the Program Manager. Using the DOS tree structure, Deus emulates the Macintosh Finder. You can open, close, and create directories, maintain windows for different directories and different drives, and run programs simply by double-clicking on their icons.

■ ■ ■ ■ ■ ■ ■ ■ ■ ■ ■ ■ ■**running the program**

When you run the Deus program, two windows appear. The first displays an icon for each drive that is on-line and readable. If you

■ Make your
Windows desktop
look like a Mac.

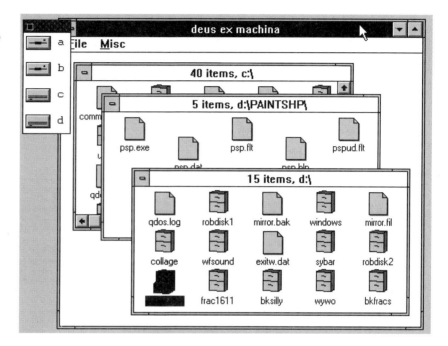

are using removable media drives, such as Bernoulli boxes, you must
have a cartridge in the drive when you first start Deus.

The second and primary window displays two pull-down main
menus and, if there are any, subordinate windows that represent
selected directories. First you see the root directory of your boot
drive. On my system, that was C:\, as you can see in the figure.
Double-click on an icon that represents a directory to display
another subordinate window and its directory/file contents.

I like the file cabinet icons that represent directories. Notice how,
when you double-click on it to open a directory, the file cabinet
icon opens its drawer. In the figure, I've opened the PAINTSHP
directory and moved the windows around. The file drawer in the
D:\ directory is now open, as is a new subordinate window that
displays the contents of the PAINTSHP directory.

As you can with the Windows Program Manager, click and drag the
icons that represent data files or directories into and out of other

subordinate windows. To copy a file or directory, select it, press and hold the Ctrl key, and drag the icon.

During any extensive move or copy operation, you can switch to another Windows program since Deus temporarily yields control to Windows in between each file transfer. If you copy lots of small files, you'll have overall system control most of the time. But if you copy large files, it is done in one shot so it will yield control back to Windows less often.

The Macintosh makes a direct provision for binding resources to a file, but Deus doesn't. Instead, Deus creates a file called DESK-TOP.DSK in each referenced subdirectory to store the information it needs. The resources that are bound include icons and descriptions. Deus creates and maintains a file, called ICONS.ALL, in the root directory of the boot drive that contains a modifiable group of icons. You can update this file and then use any of the icons to customize the Deus subordinate window, or folder, displays.

To add icons to the central ICONS.ALL file, click on any .EXE or .ICO file name that holds icons. Next, pull down the Misc menu and choose Add Icons. All icons found in that file will be copied into the ICONS.ALL file and may be used in later Deus operations.

The simplest way to use the ICONS.ALL file is to select individual icons and use them subsequently to represent a particular data file. To do this,

1   Click on the data file you wish to use. Normally, the icon is a dog-eared piece of paper. Once you select an icon, it is highlighted.

2   Select the Misc menu.

3   Choose the Set Icon command. A dialog box with a scrollable window opens. This window can successively display each icon found in the ICONS.ALL file.

4   Find the icon you want and click on OK. The icon will now be used in place of the standard paper icon for the data file you selected.

I particularly like being able to set up associations so that all files with a particular extension automatically display a specified icon. This is the chief purpose the author intended for the program. To make all files with the same extension display a specified icon,

1   Choose the Misc menu and select Icon Associations. The Icon/Extension dialog box appears.

2   What you do next depends on whether you are associating an icon with a file extension for the first time, or adjusting the icon association for an existing file extension.

   ▫   If it's the first time, click on New. The New Extension dialog box appears. Type in a three-character extension name and click on OK. The three characters you type appear in the list box at the top of the Icon/Extension dialog box.

   ▫   If you are associating for an existing file extension, open up the list box and select the desired extension from those that appear.

3   Scroll through the available icons by clicking on the arrow keys in the scroll box at the bottom of the window. When the icon you want appears, click on OK. All files with the specified extension will now use the selected icon. This will be true in all folders—that is, in all subordinate windows.

You can also bind a description to a file so that the text on the screen can be as long as forty characters instead of the eleven DOS allows. For example, instead of a typical DOS file name like Q4TH.123, you could have

Fourth Quarter, (123)

You can also run a program automatically as determined by its file extension. To do this,

1   Highlight the file name of the executable program you want to run.

2   Choose the Run Associate option in order to connect the program with files having a specific extension. A text box appears asking you to type in the extension to associate with the program.

3   Type in the extension.

That's all there is to it. Later, when you double-click on a file with the extension, the original .EXE program will open with the data file. You can associate multiple extensions with the same executable file name.

When you copy a file from one folder to another and the file has an icon bound to it, the icon will not show up in the destination folder. This happens because the icons are not bound to the file but to the DESKTOP.DSK file in each subdirectory. Deus does not update this special information file after a copy or move operation.

behind the trick

Deus was written for fun by a programmer named Scot. It is a freeware program. Scot would appreciate any comments you have, but the only way to get in touch with Scot is to address an e-mail message to him at

CompuServe: 72277,171

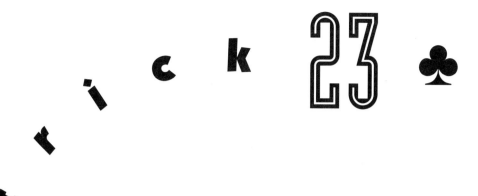

Flipper

● ● ● ● ● ● ● ● ● ● ● ● ● ● ● **the big picture**

The Flipper (FLIPPER.EXE) program is a simple printer orientation control program. Flipper displays an icon that shows you the current orientation of the default printer. If the dolphin icon is leaping in the air, it means your printer is in portrait mode. If the dolphin is swimming, your printer is in landscape mode. You can double-click on the icon to change the printer's orientation.

■ Your printer does flips when you click on this dolphin.

▪ ▪ ▪ ▪ ▪ ▪ ▪ ▪ ▪ ▪ ▪ ▪ ▪running the program

Flipper is one of several applications included in the Barry Press Utilities package. After you've completed the installation procedure, you will find a small group of Barry's programs in the BPUTILS directory.

If you occasionally—and especially if you frequently—change the orientation of your printer between landscape and portrait mode, this fun icon is for you. When the icon appears, it tells you with a glance what the current orientation of your printer is.

To change from landscape mode to portrait mode and make the dolphin stop swimming and start leaping, double-click on the icon. To switch from portrait back to landscape mode, double-click on the icon again.

This entertaining program saves you the trouble of going to the Control Panel, selecting the Printers icon, pushing the Setup button, and clicking on one of the two Orientation buttons. If for some reason you actually go through the Windows Control Panel to change printer orientation, the Flipper icon will change positions too.

The Flipper icon always shows you the orientation of the default printer. If you make a new printer the default and its orientation is different from before, the Flipper icon will change accordingly.

Some printer drivers don't respond properly to the software interface for determining and changing the printer orientation. For those drivers, Flipper displays a question mark icon to tell you it can't do its job. If this occurs, check with your printer manufacturer to see if a newer printer driver exists.

There is only one way to remove the Flipper icon from your desktop: bring up the Task Manager (press Ctrl-Esc). In the Task Manager window, highlight the name Flipper and click on the End Task button.

▫ ▫ ▫ ▫ ▫ ▫ ▫ ▫ ▫ ▫ ▫ ▫ ▫ ▫ ▫ **behind the trick**

The Flipper program is one of a larger set of programs called The Barry Press Utilities. See the Calpop trick (number 19) for more information about these utilities and their author.

Foreigner

The Foreigner (FOREIGN.EXE) program lets you include special characters that do not appear on the standard American keyboard in applications. You can copy, among other things, accented characters, fractions, superscript numbers, and symbols. You can place them directly into your Windows applications with a mouse or transmit them by way of the Clipboard.

Run the Foreigner program and the Foreigner window, shown in the figure, appears. Actually, the window you'll see is squarer than

■ Foreigner can give you the perfect French accent—and a lot more.

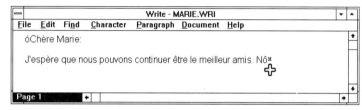

the one in the figure. I wanted you to see how Foreigner's special character window can be made to fit on a screen more efficiently.

Suppose you want to enter a copyright symbol (©) in a word-processed document. One way would be to press and hold the Alt key while typing the numbers 0169. Of course, no one can remember the numbers for all the "special" characters. An alternative for keeping track of special characters would be to make a table and keep it next to your keyboard. Of course, this still requires you to look up the number and type it in. There must be a better way. Foreigner is it!

Rather than having to remember the four-digit special character numbers, simply run Foreigner. It displays a keyboard with all the available characters in the high-ANSI and symbol character sets. Press the button with the character you want and Foreigner will copy it to the Windows Clipboard. Next, go back to your application and paste the character in from the Clipboard. (You can use either the program's Edit-Paste command or the Shift-Insert key sequence.) As you'll see shortly, you can enter special characters faster by clicking in the target application with a mouse. The character will be pasted in at the point of your click instantaneously.

You can use the current version of Foreigner without a mouse. In fact, in Windows 3.0, you have to use the arrow keys or the Tab and Shift-Tab keys to select the character you want. Windows 3.1

users can just click on the character they want, and click on the target location for the character to be pasted in. Using a mouse to select a special-character button is much easier and faster than using the keyboard.

□ □ □ □ □ □ □ □ □ □ □ □ □ □ □ **behind the trick**

Foreigner is freeware. You can freely copy it, use it, and give copies to all your friends—as long you don't modify the FOREIGN.EXE, FOREIGN.WRI, and README.TXT files. However, being freeware does not mean that Foreigner is in the public domain; Gordon retains the copyright. Do not change, edit, alter, or rename any of the files in any way. You can't fiddle with the executable program's resources either.

The author includes a long, boldface paragraph about warranties and disclaimers in his FOREIGN.WRI file. But come on, the guy has written a very neat and useful program and basically has given it away.

If you do encounter problems with Foreigner, or if you think of a way to improve it, or if you think of another Windows utility that you would find useful but cannot create yourself, feel free to contact Gordon at the addresses below.

Although he doesn't want cash for Foreigner, he is interested in hearing from people who use it. To this end, please send a postcard with a picture of your town on the front to

Gordon Goldsborough
Brandon University
Brandon, Manitoba
CANADA R7A 6A9
(204) 727-9786
FAX: (204) 726-4573
Internet: GOLDSBOROUGH@BRANDONU.CA

Bon chance!

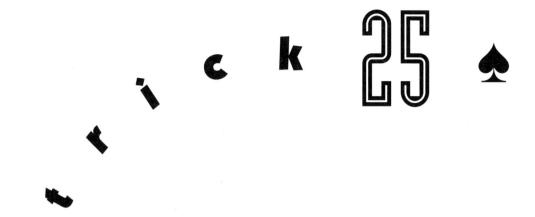

French-English Timepiece

the big picture

The French-English Timepiece (FRENCHTM.EXE) program displays the time of day in either French or English—in words of course.

running the program

Dylan Rhodes has produced an interesting variation on the digital clock. Rather than just numbers, or sweeping hour and minute hands, his program tells you the time the way you would hear it in London or Paris—in words.

■ Learn how to tell time—in French.

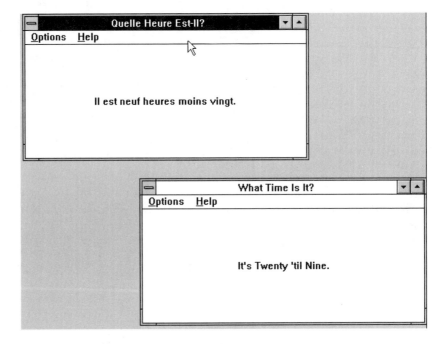

With the cooperation of one of his French friends, Dylan added a switching option that displays the time in either French or English. To change the language of the time display, just pull down the Options menu and click on the language of your choice.

Dylan has added another nice touch to his program: the time is approximated, just like a real person might do. For example, 12:53pm would come out

It's almost Five 'til One

in English, or

Il est presque une heure moins cinq

in French.

■ ■ ■ ■ ■ ■ ■ ■ ■ ■ ■ ■ ■ ■ ■ ■ **.behind the trick**

D. C. Rhodes wrote this clock program, and the French translation comes courtesy of Frederic Le Bas. The French-English Timepiece is loosely based on a program called DAYTIME that the author once saw running on a BSD Unix system.

According to the author, this program is not shareware. He says that you do not have to register it to continue using it. However, he would like it to be distributed as widely as possible. You can register the French-English Timepiece by mailing in the order form found in the WCLOCK.WRI file on-disk, or you can send $10.00 or the equivalent in non-U.S. currency to

Dylan Rhodes
P.O. Box 3215
Hayward, CA 94540-3215

Interestingly enough, you can also just contact Dylan to simply ask him to register you as a user of his program. He doesn't expect any money at all in this case. I think that he's just curious about where the path leads in the shareware world of program distribution.

Icon Catalog

•the big picture

The Icon Catalog (ICON_C) program allows you to manage your icons in a simple and intuitive way. You can group icons in special catalog files for easier reference. With that done, you can replace Windows 3.x Program Manager icons directly as well as icons in any other Windows 3.x files with the icons in the catalogs.

•running the program

When you first run the program, the main window, shown above, appears. At first no subordinate windows are visible and File is the only choice, besides the ubiquitous Help option, on the menu bar.

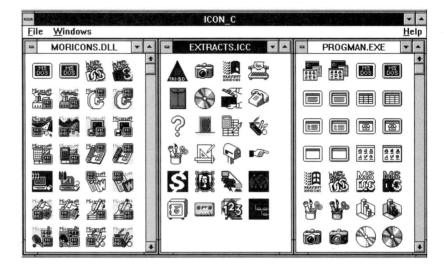

■ No more misplaced icons—put your favorites in a single icon library.

Select File and select Open in order to select a disk file that may contain icons. At this point, the File menu only offers three obvious choices: New, Open, and Exit. Select New to start grouping your own new catalog.

Select Open to open up existing files and discover what icons lie within them. You can explore the contents of any disk file whatsoever. The program does offer special buttons for opening files with .ICC (the catalog files created by this program), .ICO, .EXE, and .DLL extensions.

In the figure, I selected Open twice to open up the MORICONS.DLL and the PROGMAN.EXE files. Then I used the New choice to create an EXTRACTS.ICC catalog file. Initiating a new catalog file with the New choice can be slightly confusing because a dialog box opens up that asks for the ICC name you would like to "save." Just type in the name you would like to use. The program will use that name when it saves your work later on.

Once you've created a subordinate window, a new Windows menu appears and menu choices—Save, Save As, Close, and File Properties—appear on the File menu. You can continue to open existing files and discover icons for your new library file. In my example,

I collected a number of interesting icons from several existing disk files for my library file, and I named it EXTRACTS.ICC (see the figure).

The File Properties command shows the properties of a file, including its file name, file type, date last saved, the size of the file in bytes, number of icons in the file, and number of icons currently in the window. Use the File Properties command to keep track of how many icons you added to the file during this session and when you last made changes to the file, and to manage your icon catalogs.

Once you've opened several subordinate windows, use standard Windows techniques to drag icons from other files into your new ICC file. You can also use Copy and Move techniques with your mouse to group and regroup icon collections in several different ICC files. Remember to use the Save or Save As choices on the File menu before you exit from the Icon Catalog. Now let's take a closer look at the various control possibilities.

■ ■ ■ ■ ■ ■ ■ ■ ■ ■ ■ ■ ■ ■ **adding new icons**

The program uses the file extension .ICC to represent icon catalog files. These files are special in that the program recognizes them as catalogs for icons. Because it knows that they are catalogs of icons, it allows you to add icons to the file. You are only allowed to add icons to .ICC files.

There are four steps to the procedure. First you create a new .ICC file, which is called the catalog file. Then you open a file, called the source file, that contains Windows icons. Then you select an icon from the source file and drag it to the catalog file. Finally, you save the changes you made to the catalog file.

1   First you create a new .ICC file. Go to the ICON_C menu and select the File/New option. A dialog box appears. Here you specify the name you want to give to your

catalog. You may also change the directory that you will keep it in. After you enter a name and a path if desired, click on the Save As button. The new catalog file is created with a single place-holder icon in it. This is the TRI-S D logo icon for the company that makes the Icon Catalog.

2   You need to open a file with the Windows icons you want to copy. Select the File/Open option to bring up the dialog box. Here you search through the directories for a file that contains icons you want to copy. Let's say you want to copy the icons from the ICON_C.EXE file. Select the File Type by clicking on the *.EXE button. Next, go to the directory with the ICON_C.EXE file by selecting the appropriate entries in the Directories list box. Remember, you can select a list box entry by double-clicking on it. Next, double-click on the ICON_C.EXE entry in the Files list box to open it.

3   The catalog and source file are open. To copy an icon from the source file, move the cursor over the icon you want and hold down the left mouse button. Do not let go of the button. Notice that the icon is now selected and the cursor is the shape of the icon. Move the icon to the catalog file and release the mouse button.

4   Save the changes you have made to the catalog with the File/Save option from the menu.

changing program manager icons

One of this program's best features is that it allows you to replace program item icons in a Windows 3.0 Program Manager group directly. You'll have to contact the author for an update to the software that performs this unique task under Windows 3.1. All you have to do is select an icon from an ICON_C catalog file, and drag and drop it over the program item icon you want to change. This way you bypass the awkward method required by the Program Manager. Actually, you can use any file type supported by ICON_C as the source file for the replacement icon!

There are three steps to replacing a program item icon. First you open the file with the new icon, called the source file. Next you open the Program Manager program group that contains the icon you want to replace. This is called the destination icon. Finally you select the new icon from the source file, drag it over the destination icon, and drop it.

Sometimes you will get a message saying that the transfer could not be completed because of incompatible icon types. This occurs when you try to replace a monochrome, or black-and-white, icon with a colored one. The only way to get around this particular problem is to use the Program Manager to change the icon.

▪ ▪ ▪ ▪ ▪ ▪ ▪ ▪ ▪ ▪ ▪ replacing icons in a file

You can replace any Windows 3.x icon with another icon. Normally you do this to change an icon in one of your .ICC files. This way, you can simulate deleting an icon from an .ICC file. You cannot delete icons from .ICC files directly with the current release of the Icon Catalog.

Suppose you want to replace an icon in an executable program with one of your favorite icons. You can do this, but not with all programs because of copy protection and anti-virus schemes. Therefore, it is a good idea to make a backup copy of any program whose icon you want to change. If you are using an active anti-virus program, you may have to let it know you are changing an executable program file. See your anti-virus program manual for information about this.

There are four steps to replacing an icon. First you open the .ICC file, called the source file, with the new icon. Any file can be used as the source file! Next you open the file with the Windows icon you want to replace. This is called the destination file. You then select the new icon from the source file and drag it to the destination file. Finally, you save the changes made to the destination file.

creating a backup file

Backing up a file simply means saving it in a different place under a different name. Backups let you make changes to a file and still keep a copy of the original. You will want to do this when you are changing the icons in any executable file type—that is, a program.

There are only two steps to creating a backup file:

1 Open the file you want to back up with the File/Open command.

2 Save the file under a different name, and directory if you want, with the File/Save As command. Now you can make changes to the new file and it will not affect the original.

If you are renaming an executable file, you must still keep its .EXE extension or you will not be able to run it later. For example, if you were renaming ICON_C.EXE, you would call it NEW_ICC.EXE instead of ICON_C.NEW. Also, you can't use a *.DLL file normally after you change its name.

error messages

There are several types of error messages. Most of them appear when memory or disk space is very low. The following describes the error messages and what should be done when you encounter them.

Error message—Memory "A memory error occurred. Please reduce system memory usage before trying again." When this message is displayed, an operation was attempted but could not be completed because not enough system memory was available. If you get this message, close one or more applications before you try to perform the same operation again.

Error message—File/Disk   "A file error occurred. You have either deleted a file used by ICON_C or you have run out of disk space. Please check disk/file condition before proceeding." This message occurs because either you ran out of disk space while trying to save a file, or you deleted a file with the File Manager or DOS and ICON_C thought it still existed. If you ran out of disk space, you need to run the File Manager and delete unnecessary files. Or you can choose the Save As command and save the file to a different disk drive. If you deleted the file, there is not much that can be done. ICON_C cannot reproduce the file if it has been deleted, even though the icons are still shown on the screen. This is because ICON_C does not copy all file information when it is run. It only copies the icon information necessary to display the icon. Do not delete a file that ICON_C is currently using!

Error message—Critical Memory Error   "A critical memory error occurred. This window has to be closed. Please reduce system memory usage before proceeding." This error message occurs when ICON_C becomes confused. It usually happens because not enough system memory is available. The window had to be closed and all changes made to it have been lost. The only thing to do now is to close down unnecessary applications and try over again.

supported file types

ICON_C supports the following file formats:

- ◻ *.ICC—ICON_C specific file format for the icon catalog (or library). This is the only file type to which you can add icons.

- *.ICO—Standard Windows 3.x icon file format.

- *.EXE—An executable file. Generally, only Windows 3.0 files of this type have icons that ICON_C can understand. Note, however, that executable files are not always Windows 3.x executable files. Some are for DOS and some are for earlier versions of Windows. Normally, these files will not contain icons, and ICON_C will not be able to understand them even if they do. ICON_C does not support these other executable files. Some executable files run in Windows 3.x but do not contain Windows 3.x format icons. These hybrid file types—most notably Microsoft Excel and Microsoft Word for Windows—are not supported by ICON_C.

- *.DLL—Dynamic Link Library files. These are similar in format to Windows executable files and may contain icons.

supported icon types

Windows 3.x supports icons of 2, 8, and 16 colors. It also supports icons of various pixel lengths—16, 32, and 64—because some combinations look better on different display types. When a Windows 3.x executable file type is opened under ICON_C, you will often see three icons that look quite similar. These icons are for different display types. Windows only displays the one that looks best for your current display. ICON_C supports, and displays, all three icon types.

There are two limitations to keep in mind. If you replace an icon of one color and resolution with an icon of a different color or resolution, ICON_C changes the format of the replacement icon to match the original icon. This conversion is made automatically. The resulting icon may not look as good as the original if it was changed to a lower resolution or it has fewer colors.

You cannot replace Program Manager icons with icons of different colors or resolutions. They must match exactly. ICON_C will not make the automatic conversion if they don't.

∎ ∎ ∎ ∎ ∎ ∎ ∎ ∎ ∎ ∎ ∎ ∎ ∎ ∎ ∎ ∎ **behind the trick**

If you have any questions or comments about this program, please send them to

Tri-S Designs
112 Westbrook Hills Drive
Syracuse, NY 13215-1820

The Icon Catalog program is shareware, and was written and copyrighted by Dominick P. Calabria. You may use this program for a 30 day trial period. If at the end of the 30 days you do not like the program, just stop using it. If you like the program and would like to continue using it, you must register it. When you do you will receive the latest version of ICON_C with all registration nag screens disabled. To register, send $15.00 to Tri-S Designs at the above address. Please say whether you want 5¼" or 3½" disks.

Feel free to copy and share this shareware version of ICON_C. The only stipulation is that all three files—ICON_C.EXE, ICON_C.HLP, and README.TXT—are kept together and not altered. All resulting copies are still copyrighted shareware and require registration in accordance with the above paragraph.

Lock

the big picture

The Lock (LOCK.EXE) program from METZ Software is a security application for Microsoft Windows. It protects your system from user access via the mouse or keyboard. While the keyboard and mouse are locked, other applications are free to continue executing.

running the program

Lock cannot prevent someone from rebooting or powering off your machine, but it will prevent them from accessing your machine via the keyboard or mouse. Check with METZ software for their latest version of Lock. They have a significantly more powerful version,

◘ Better than kryptonite for protecting your system while you are away.

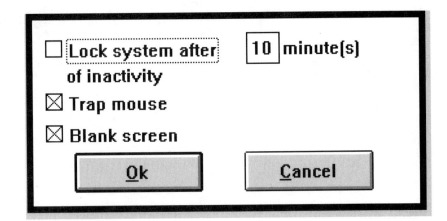

but it is four times the size of this one, and I couldn't fit it on the disk that comes with this book.

Lock appears on your screen as an icon in the form of a keyhole. Click on the Lock Icon with either the left or right mouse button to display the System menu. Choose Lock here to instantly blank your screen, once you've configured Lock to the extent of knowing your password. Alternatively, you can always press Ctrl-L from any Windows screen—that is, not from within a DOS application—to instantly lock your system.

Because Lock is password-driven, it can't perform until you have gone through the password entry procedure at least once. Lock uses a careful double-entry method that requires you to enter and reenter, for confirmation purposes, a multicharacter password. Even if you forget at first to use the Set Password option on the System menu, Lock will take you through it automatically the first time you attempt to lock your system.

Once you've established the password, Lock will continue to use it until you change passwords. You can access all of Lock's menu commands from its System menu.

If you choose to run Lock from a command line—that is, in the File Manager, Program Manager, or from one of this book's programs like Runner—you may use one or both of two helpful command line switches, /H and /L.

◘ /H hides the Lock icon so that no one can tell that your system has a locking capability. If you use the /H switch to hide the Lock icon when you run the program, you have to configure the Inactivity option, or else Lock will not be effective when its icon is hidden.

◘ /L locks the system automatically when you initially run the Lock program.

Lock also lets you make the screen go blank while your system is locked. Select Blank screen from the Configure dialog box. Lock will automatically center the password dialog boxes on your screen and beep when an invalid password is entered.

The Configure menu, located on the System menu, offers three choices.

◘ **Lock system after** lets you lock the system automatically after a certain period of time without the keyboard or mouse being active. Place an *X* in the first check box and enter the number of minutes of inactivity you want to pass before locking occurs. You can set a value between 1 and 60 minutes of keyboard and mouse inactivity. If you do not check the Lock system after box, locking only occurs when you explicitly request it.

◘ **Trap Mouse** confines the mouse to the Lock dialog box when your system is locked.

◘ **Blank Screen** is a toggle that determines whether the entire screen is blacked out during a system locking period. Place an *X* in this box if you want the screen to black out when locking is initiated. The System Locked dialog box will appear in the middle of the screen when Lock detects keyboard or mouse activity. At that time, you have to enter your password and press Enter to regain control of your Windows system. If you don't place an *X* in the Blank Screen box, the screen will not black out during locking. Instead, the System Locked dialog box will appear in the center of the screen when you move the mouse. It will remain there, along with all other windows and icons, until you correctly enter the right password.

▪ ▪ ▪ ▪ ▪ ▪ ▪ ▪ ▪ ▪ ▪ ▪ ▪ ▪ ▪ ▪ **behind the trick**

Art Metz, the founder of METZ Software, is responsible for the Lock program and for several other commercial and shareware programs. You can reach his company at

METZ Software
P.O. Box 6699
Bellevue, WA 98008-0699
(206) 641-4525 (support)
(800) 447-1712 (sales)
(206) 644-6026 (FAX)
CompuServe: 75300,1627
GEnie: A.METZ

Mouse Cursor Changer

▪ ▪ ▪ ▪ ▪ ▪ ▪ ▪ ▪ ▪ ▪ ▪ ▪ ▪ ▪ ▪ ▪ the big picture

This package permanently changes the shape of the system default mouse pointer. The program calls the mouse pointer a "cursor." The original cursor setup is preserved and can be restored later by running a batch file.

▪ ▪ ▪ ▪ ▪ ▪ ▪ ▪ ▪ ▪ ▪ ▪ ▪ ▪ running the program

Individual applications sometimes change the shape of the mouse cursor under Windows 3.x, but the system default cursor is always the traditional right-handed arrow. Applications sometimes use the

■ The curse of the boring cursor has ended. Change it to something more entertaining.

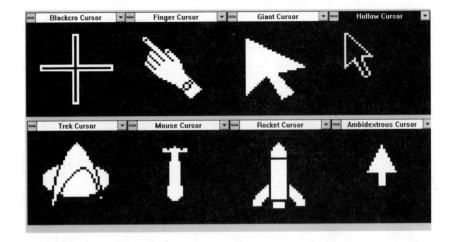

debugging hook functions in Windows to temporarily alter the system default cursor, but altering it this way has one particular disadvantage: the program that has changed the cursor must remain running for the cursor to keep its new shape.

This program works by creating a duplicate display driver file that overwrites the internally coded cursor bitmap with your new, user-selected bitmap. In other words, the cursor you select overwrites the default cursor. The cursor "hotspot" is adjusted also. The hotspot is the place, usually at the tip of the traditional arrow pointer, that is tested to determine if a mouse click has fallen on a menu item, a button, and so on.

Farpoint Software has designed this package to protect your system. The cursor changing program adjusts your SYSTEM.INI file to use the new display driver that is created during the following process. Your system's original display driver is not touched, and your original SYSTEM.INI is renamed SYSTEM.BAK. The cursor changing program creates a batch file called RESETCSR.BAT, which can be run in order to later restore the original SYSTEM.INI and delete the duplicate display driver.

To change your mouse pointer's shape, follow these steps:

1   Run the CHOOSCUR.EXE program located in the \SYBEX\NEWCSR directory.

2   A Directory Selection dialog box appears. Enter the complete path name to your NEWCSR directory. For example, if your root drive is C:, you would enter

   C:\SYBEX\NEWCSR

   and choose OK.

3   The Cursor Selector window appears. It contains a list box with the names of all the cursor (*.CUR) files in the specified directory. Now you can look at the many cursor alternatives. Click on each cursor name and the mouse cursor changes to the cursor shape defined by the .CUR file.

4   Once you've chosen a cursor shape, use it to pull down the File menu in the Cursor Selector window. Choose the Prepare Batch File option from the File menu. The program creates two batch files named SETCSR.BAT and RESETCSR.BAT in the specified C:\SYBEX\NEWCSR directory.

5   You must exit Windows. This step is very important because it alters the Windows SYSTEM.INI initialization file in preparation for restarting Windows with the new mouse pointer you chose. From the DOS prompt, switch to the appropriate NEWCSR directory (C:\SYBEX\NEWCSR).

6   Run SETCSR.BAT by simply typing SETCSR at the prompt. This will create two new files, one in the Windows SYSTEM directory named NDISPLAY.DRV that will be the new display driver, and one in the WINDOWS directory named SYSTEM.BAK that will be kept as a copy of the

original SYSTEM.INI. Note that SETCSR.BAT makes use of two other programs that are included in the CHGCSR directory, NEWCSR.EXE and CHANGINI.EXE.

7 Restart Windows. The cursor you selected should now be the default cursor.

If you decide later on to restore the original cursor shape, you can do so easily with the following steps:

1 Exit from Windows. Again, it is very important to run the batch files involved here from the DOS prompt rather than from a Windows DOS session prompt.

2 Switch to the directory that contains the cursor and batch files (C:\SYBEX\NEWCSR).

3 Run RESETCSR.BAT. The original SYSTEM.INI is restored from the SYSTEM.BAK copy that you made during the modification procedure. The adjusted NDISPLAY.DRV driver is deleted as well.

4 Restart Windows.

If you are short on disk space, you can erase everything in the C:\SYBEX\NEWSCSR directory once you've chosen a new cursor. The only file you really need to restore the original cursor is RESETCSR.BAT. This batch file is only a convenience—it just copies SYSTEM.BAK to SYSTEM.INI, and deletes SYSTEM.BAK and NDISPLAY.DRV.

The cursor files included in this package are interesting. A total of 25 cursors come with this package.

▪ ▪ ▪ ▪ ▪ ▪ ▪ ▪ ▪ ▪ ▪ ▪ ▪ ▪ ▪ ▪ behind the trick

Mouse Cursor Changer is written and copyrighted by Farpoint Software. It has been released as freeware. It is, however, still copyrighted material. It may be freely copied and distributed, provided that all the files in the original archive are distributed together and that no fee is charged except for a disk duplication fee not to exceed $5.00. The program may not be included as an item bundled with other software or hardware and sold for profit.

The user of the Mouse Cursor Changer assumes all risk. The programs in this package are provided as-is without warranty of any kind. Although care has been taken to assure proper operation of these programs, bugs may exist. The program worked quite well for me and I encountered no problems in my tests.

If you like (or dislike) this program, the author would appreciate your comments, suggestions, or proposals for other freeware or shareware programs. If you would like the full source code for this package, it is available for $20.00 from

Farpoint Software
2501 Afton Court
League City, Texas 77573
CompuServe: 74030,554 (to Alan Jones)

Periodic Table

▪ ▪ ▪ ▪ ▪ ▪ ▪ ▪ ▪ ▪ ▪ ▪ ▪ ▪ ▪ ▪ ▪.the big picture

The Periodic Table (PERIODIC.EXE) program depicts the Periodic Table of the Elements. Click on any element to display a large window with many interesting facts about each element, including which group it belongs to, its atomic weight, and its date of discovery.

▪ ▪ ▪ ▪ ▪ ▪ ▪ ▪ ▪ ▪ ▪ ▪ ▪.running the program

Run the program and you will see a maximized window with the Periodic Table of the Elements. Each small box has an element symbol in the center, its atomic number in the upper-left corner, and depending on which type of detail you chose, some additional

■ It's elementary, my dear Watson.

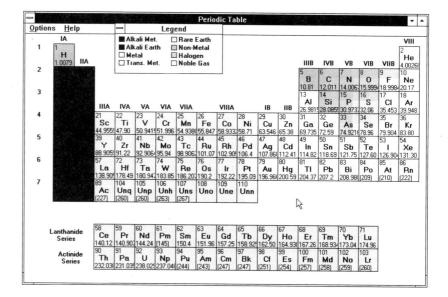

data along the bottom. The element's atomic weight is shown by default. A legend window at the top of the screen shows what the different colors in the table represent.

The command menu for the Periodic Table is very simple. There are two menu items, Options and Help. The Options menu has three commands of its own: Set, Save, and Exit. Choose Set and you will see a complex dialog box with many optional control settings. For example, one list box allows you to choose which font you want to see in the main Periodic Table. All installed Windows fonts appear in this list box.

You can change the colors that represent the different groups in the Legend box—Metal, Rare Earth, and so on. To do this, choose the group name you want from the list box and specify the combination of red, green, and blue (from 0 to 255) that you wish to represent the elements of a particular type.

You can turn the Legend box on or off by placing or removing the check mark beside the Legend choice in the dialog box. The Legend box determines the color coding scheme. You can change the color coding to depict not only the elements by group, but by date of discovery or isolation, or by temperature (gas, liquid, or solid). Specify which of these display modes to use by clicking once on a button in the Mode section to the right of the Options dialog box.

You can also choose which set of details to display at the bottom of the element boxes. To do this, click on one of the five buttons—atomic weight, electrons, shells, electronegativity, or the atomic radius—in the Detail section in the middle of the Options dialog box.

Once you've configured the program to display the Periodic Table in the way you would like to see it, pull down the Options menu and select Save. All the settings you chose in the Options dialog box will be saved in the WIN.INI file.

Naturally, the Exit command closes the Periodic Table window. The Help menu has three standard and obvious commands—Index, Help, and About.

- **Index** displays the Help index for the Periodic Table.

- **Help** displays Windows help information about how to use the help system.

- **About** displays the copyright box for the Periodic Table. This command is also available from the System menu.

behind the trick

Contact the authors of this program at

SMI Enterprises Corp.
P.O. Box 582221
Tulsa, OK 74158
(918) 560-9536

The authors chose a two-tier approach to licensing the program. First, it is a shareware program and you are granted a 30 day trial license. If you use the program and like it, you have to pay a license fee to continue using the program.

Second, if you would like to see the code that makes it work, you can pay a slightly higher license fee and get all the source files needed to build the PERIODIC.EXE program. This includes all the icon, bitmap, RC, dialog, and DEF files. In addition, you also get all the source files needed to build the PERIODIC.HLP file. Plus, you get a file in Windows Write format that explains certain sections of the program in more detail than the program comments do.

Read the disk documentation that accompanies the product for further registration and source code information. If you wish to license either the executable or the source code versions, please use the appropriate order form in the PERIODIC.WRI file.

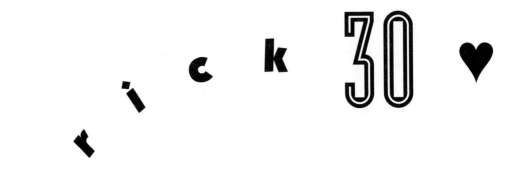

t r i c k 30 ♥

Runner

● ■ ■ ■ ■ ■ ■ ■ ■ ■ ■ ■ ■ ■ ■ **.the big picture**

The Runner (RUNNER.EXE) program offers an easy and quick way to run any command line or execute any program. Just click on the runner's foot icon to bring up the figure shown here. You can type any command line into the entry field. This function works like the File/Run command in the Program Manager.

■ In one small step, you'll be leaps ahead.

Enter command line:	Ok	Cancel	❯
write|			

running the program

This Runner program is one of several applications included in the Barry Press Utilities package. After you complete the installation procedure, you will find a small group of Barry's programs in the BPUTILS directory. Register one of these programs with Barry and he will send you his much larger set of application utilities.

When you start this program, an icon that looks like a runner's foot appears on your desktop. All you have to do is click on the icon to run any Windows or DOS program, or to initiate the command line prepared as part of a .PIF file. For DOS batch files, you can either type the name of the batch file itself or set up a customized .PIF and incorporate the batch file as the command line to execute when you run the .PIF. You can enter the name of a non-Windows application or a DOS batch file and Runner will initiate a DOS session and run the specified program within it. With this method, you can run or test a DOS application program or the contents of a batch file quickly.

To remove the Runner icon from your desktop, bring up the Task Manager (press Ctrl-Esc). In the Task Manager window, highlight the name Runner and click on the End Task button. This is the only way you can remove the Runner icon.

behind the trick

The Runner program is one of a larger set of programs called The Barry Press Utilities. See the Calpop trick (number 19) for more information about these utilities and their author.

trick 31 ♣

S top

. . . . the big picture

The Stop (STOP.EXE) program displays a red STOP sign icon. Click on it once to exit Windows. Clicking this icon is the same as switching to the Program Manager and selecting File/Exit from its Main menu bar.

■ It's the 5:00 whistle. Time to go home.

▫ ▫ ▫ ▫ ▫ ▫ ▫ ▫ ▫ ▫ ▫ ▫ ▫ running the program

Once Stop is up and running, you can exit both Windows and all open Windows applications simply by clicking on the red STOP icon.

One of Windows' nicest features is its ability to communicate between tasks. Stop takes advantage of this. Essentially, it requests all open applications to close themselves, at which time each application executes its own shut-down procedure. For instance, a program with an open file you have modified will ask you to save the file before exiting.

▫ ▫ ▫ ▫ ▫ ▫ ▫ ▫ ▫ ▫ ▫ ▫ ▫ ▫ behind the trick

Stop is distributed as shareware by Michael Gracer. If you like Stop and continue to use it, please send a $5.00 registration fee to

Michael Gracer
Digital Simulations
46 Dublin Road
Southbury, CT 06488

Stopwatch

◾ ◾ ◾ ◾ ◾ ◾ ◾ ◾ ◾ ◾ ◾ ◾ ◾ ◾ ◾ ◾ ◾ the big picture

The Stopwatch (SW.EXE) program is a computerized stopwatch and clock.

◾ ◾ ◾ ◾ ◾ ◾ ◾ ◾ ◾ ◾ ◾ ◾ ◾ ◾ ◾ running the program

After you start the SW.EXE program, you can time an event by selecting the Start/Stop button with the mouse or by pressing the Enter key. When the event is over, select the Start/Stop button or press the Enter key again. To save times while the stopwatch is running, select the Save button.

■ Use your $2000 Windows computer as a $10 stopwatch.

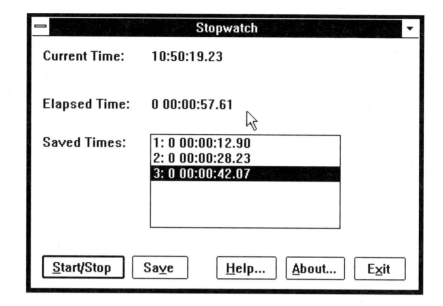

The current time is always displayed in a 24-hour format, as follows:

hour:minutes:seconds.hundredths of one second

Elapsed times are displayed as

days:hours:minutes:seconds.hundredths of one second

To get help while the program is running, select the Help button with the mouse. To obtain information about the program—its version number or copyright—select the About button. To quit the program, select the Exit Program button with the mouse.

■ ■ ■ ■ ■ ■ ■ ■ ■ ■ ■ ■ ■ ■ ■ ■ **behind the trick**

The Stopwatch program may be freely copied without cost, provided it is not changed in any way. If you find the program useful, send $5.00 to

Pocket-Sized Software
8547 East Arapahoe Road
Suite J-147
Greenwood Village, CO 80112

WorldTime

∎ ∎ ∎ ∎ ∎ ∎ ∎ ∎ ∎ ∎ ∎ ∎ ∎ ∎ ∎ **the big picture**

The WorldTime (WTIME.EXE) program displays the local time, Greenwich mean time, and the time in the five continental U.S. time zones. In addition, two controls you select display the current time in two of 110 metropolitan and geographic locations around the world. Finally, you can display the time in a location of your own choosing. All configuration settings can be saved, so each is in effect whenever you run the program.

◘ "What time is it?"
now comes in
international flavors.

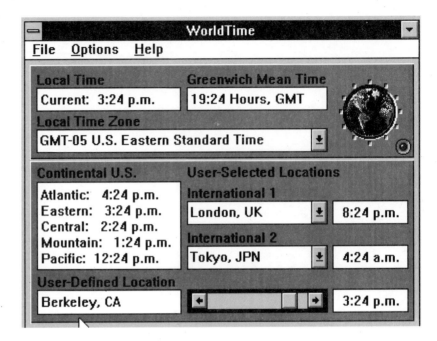

running the program

The main program file, WTIME.EXE, obtains the configuration information from a file called WTIME.INI each time you run the program. Each time you exit the program, any changes you made to configuration are written to WTIME.INI. For this reason, both files should be stored in the same directory when you run WorldTime from a hard drive.

The setup and configuration for WorldTime are fairly straightforward. The most important thing to do before you run WorldTime is to make sure your computer's system clock—its DOS Time and Date—settings are accurate. Do this from the DOS prompt with the TIME and DATE commands, by means of a setup utility, or with Windows itself by using the Control Panel.

For WorldTime to function correctly, you must select your local time zone in the Local Time Zone list box. Once this is done, all WorldTime calculations will be based on your computer's system clock relative to Greenwich mean time (GMT). The local time zone selection need only be made once, unless you move your computer to a different time zone, of course.

All configuration settings are saved to the WTIME.INI file when you exit WorldTime, but changes to the configuration are saved to the WTIME.INI file only if you exit with the File/Exit command sequence. Closing WorldTime by double-clicking on the control button in the upper-left corner or by pressing the Alt-F4 key combination does not save WorldTime's current or new settings.

daylight savings time mode

WorldTime has a user-enabled Daylight Savings Time (DST) mode. If Daylight Savings Time is in effect in your time zone, run the program in DST mode. Toggle DST mode on or off with the Options/DST Mode selection on the menu bar. When Daylight Savings Time mode is on, or active, WorldTime makes the necessary adjustments to all time displays. Once again, this assumes that your computer system clock is set to the right time.

You can tell when DST mode is active because you'll see a Red indicator to the right of the WorldTime globe logo. WorldTime knows when Daylight Savings Time periods are in effect in different parts of the world, and it handles them itself without the user having to be involved.

Daylight Savings Time is officially observed in the United States from the first Sunday in April to the last Sunday in October. Even so, certain places in the U.S. and its territories do not observe Daylight Savings Time. For example, Arizona, Hawaii, parts of

Indiana, the Commonwealth of Puerto Rico, and the Virgin Islands don't observe it.

Many countries in the world observe Daylight Savings Time, but the dates of observance differ from nation to nation. In the case of some countries in the Southern Hemisphere, Daylight Savings Time occurs at the opposite time of year to our Daylight Savings Time.

WorldTime recognizes the Daylight Savings Time periods observed in all the nations listed in the User-Selected Location controls, but for it to do so the time and date settings of your computer's system clock must be correct.

The Greenwich Mean Time display always shows true Standard Time at the Prime Meridian, even when locations in that time zone are observing Daylight Savings Time. For this reason, the Greenwich Mean Time display will sometimes differ from clock times shown for locations like London and Manchester that lie in the Greenwich mean time zone.

In some countries, the official policy concerning Daylight Savings Time is flexible and subject to periodic change. Future releases of WorldTime will attempt to take account of such changes.

▫ ▫ ▫ ▫ ▫ ▫ ▫ ▫ ▫ ▫ ▫ ▫ ▫ ▫ ▫ behind the trick

WorldTime is shareware, not freeware. It was created by Pegasus Development. Product registration is necessary if companies like Pegasus are to continue providing quality software for the shareware marketplace. Registration entitles you to upgrade and update information for WorldTime, as well as the other new titles in the company's product line.

Product support and upgrade information are available only to registered users. Full registration information can be found in the

WTIME.TXT file in your \SYBEX\WORLDTIM directory. To become a registered user, send a check or money-order for $10.00 to

Pegasus Development
WorldTime (1.1) Registration
11900 Grant Place
Des Peres, Missouri 63131
(314) 256-3130 (local St. Louis)
(800) 788-0787 (orders only)

PART........

3

spellbound

Some programs, like some products, aren't particularly functional. But you wouldn't give them up for anything. For example, did you ever own a kaleidoscope, a spirograph, or a lava lamp? The programs in this section are similar to these types of products.

When you run them, you'll be able to sit back and enjoy the show. In one program, a world of atomic movements will delight you. In another, a fractal landscape will colorfully and three-dimensionally appear before your very eyes. There are programs to let you see stars, play familiar musical scores through your PC's speaker, and even practice your own version of meditation in case you need to take a break from the other magic tricks in this book.

trick 34 ♥

Atoms

■ ■ ■ ■ ■ ■ ■ ■ ■ ■ ■ ■ ■ ■ ■ ■ ■ .the big picture

The Atoms (ATOMS.EXE) program, a computer-generated art program, offers a range of colors and patterns to captivate you. You'll spend a lot of time gazing and glazing in front of your computer screen. The author says that the program is useless and a great way to waste time. The program generates random color changes with basic pixel, rectangle, and ellipse graphic figures.

■ ■ ■ ■ ■ ■ ■ ■ ■ ■ ■ ■ ■ ■ ■ ■ .running the program

This program offers the conventional series of Windows menus for controlling all aspects of the art it generates. Personally, I found the

■ Exploring atomic evolution in a miniature universe.

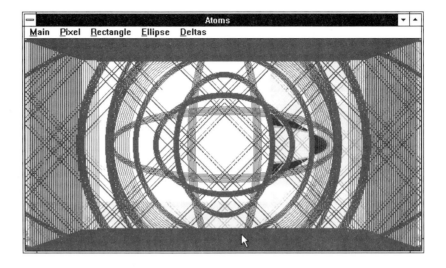

program most engaging when I just pulled down each menu and made new choices at random. The terminology on the menus can be elusive, but the multicolored patterns that appear in the window are easy to recognize and very pleasing.

Naturally, you can change the size of the Atoms window and enjoy its colorful patterns while you work in another window. When you minimize the program, it continues to paint pictures on its icon. This special touch appealed to me. Everybody's icon parking lot at the bottom of the Windows screen is beginning to fill up. In the same way I like animated wallpaper, I like it when icons take on a life of their own.

As to the menus, try the choices on the Pixel menu to obtain interesting technical effects. The Rectangle and Ellipse menu generate clear, solid, or combination graphics by creating different curves with either sharp or soft circumferences. The Delta menu controls the skews and color rate changes. Your choices here will modify one at a time the x or y screen positions at which various pixels are illuminated, as well as the colors used for illuminating the window.

▪ ▪ ▪ ▪ ▪ ▪ ▪ ▪ ▪ ▪ ▪ ▪ ▪ ▪ ▪ ▪ **behind the trick**

Atoms is shareware and is copyrighted by AK–SYS. No kidding. If you like it, use it and pass it along freely. No trial period, no nagware, and no requirements whatsoever stand between you and the use of this program.

If you like Atoms and wish to register it, send any amount at all to

> AK–SYS
> 1514 Selby Road
> Naperville, IL 60563

When you register Atoms, AK-SYS adds your name to its user database. You will be kept informed of updates and the gee-whiz software that they make available. If your contribution covers the cost (probably at least $10.00), they will mail the latest iteration and enhancement to you on the diskette size you specify. Use the registration form in the ATOMS.DOC file in your SYBEX\ATOMS directory.

Fractal Viewer

The Fractal Viewer (FRACVIEW.EXE) program displays a graphical rendition of the Mandelbrot set (a beautiful fractal geometric image). You, the user, can zoom in on whatever region of the image most interests you.

Run the program and it will begin drawing a colorful fractal picture. The Fractal Viewer uses a compatible math co-processor if one is

◘ It looks like an ink-blot test, but it's really fractal geometry.

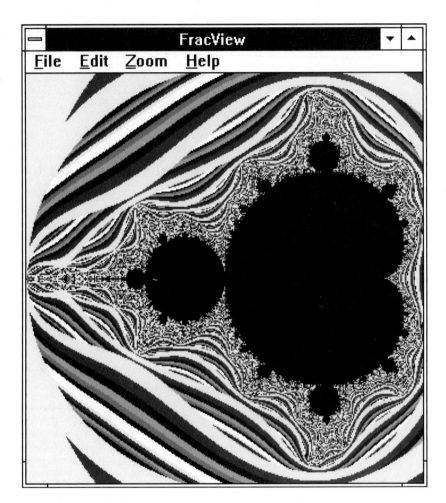

installed on your computer. A math co-processor is highly recommended, because the program takes its sweet time to draw an image. Nearly all programs that generate fractal images are very slow for the same reason: the mathematical computations necessary to compute color patterns on the screen steal a considerable amount of CPU time.

Use the following keys to perform special tasks while the program is generating its image:

F1	activates the Help system.
F2	zooms in on a new region of interest.
F3	zooms out to the previous region of interest.
Ctrl-Insert	copies the screen image to the Clipboard so you can paste it into other programs.

The program offers four menu bar options: File, Edit, Zoom, and Help. To activate these menu choices, either click on them or press Alt-F, Alt-E, Alt-Z, or Alt-H respectively.

The File menu offers only one choice, Exit. Select this option when you wish to quit the program. The Edit menu likewise offers only one choice, Copy. Use it after your fractal image has finished generating. Select Copy (or press Ctrl-Insert) and the current screen image is copied to the Clipboard at whatever zoom level you're in. From there, you can paste it into other programs.

Press F2 or click on the Zoom In choice to zoom into a new region of interest (ROI) in the fractal image that's displayed. To select a new ROI,

1 Move the mouse to one corner of the ROI.

2 Press the left mouse button and drag the mouse to the opposite corner. The ROI will be highlighted in inverse video.

3 Release the left mouse button.

4 Now that you've selected the ROI, choose the Zoom In command to make the ROI fill the entire drawing window.

Press F3 or click on the Zoom Out choice to zoom out to the previous region of interest.

■ ■ ■ ■ ■ ■ ■ ■ ■ ■ ■ ■ ■ ■ ■ ■ **behind the trick**

This Fractal Viewer program may be freely copied without cost, provided it is not changed in any way. If you find the program useful, send $5.00 to

Pocket-Sized Software
8547 East Arapahoe Road
Suite J-147
Greenwood Village, CO 80112

Kaleidoscope

the big picture

Remember how much fun it was to look into the cylindrical tube of a kaleidoscope and turn the barrel? Shifting colors appeared, refracted through the many pieces of glass inside. The Kaleidoscope (KALDEMO.EXE) program saves you the wrist-ache of turning the kaleidoscope yourself. The program creates an infinite sequence of colorful patterns.

running the program

Run the program one or more times to discover how captivating a kaleidoscope display can be. In each Kal window, as you can see

■ Lose yourself in the symmetrical shifting shapes and colors.

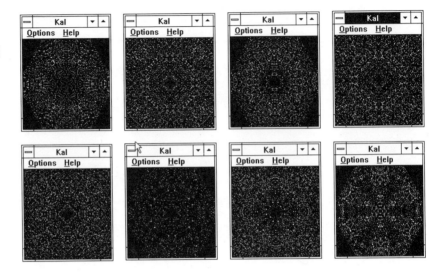

in the figure, there is an Options and Help pull-down menu. You control the display and creation settings from the Options menu. From the Help menu you can receive on-line help about all options. Personally, I like running the program eight times to create the computer equivalent to a set of stained-glass windows.

In my demo version, all the settings and controls are not activated. You have to register the program with its author to receive a complete working copy and make all possible changes. You'll find information about contacting the author in the About box, which is located under the Help pull-down menu.

The Kaleidoscope program can be used as a very attractive screen-saver. Just pull down the Options menu and place a check mark beside the Screen Saver choice. The demo version comes with a built-in timer that activates the screen-saver. To clear the animated screen saver from your screen, just move the mouse.

Click on the Pause choice on the Options menu when you want to freeze a kaleidoscopic image, either to capture it for a book or presentation, or just to admire it. Click on Pause once again to reactivate the kaleidoscopic animation.

The Square option controls the degree of symmetry that is generated. Place a check mark beside Square and Kaleidoscope will use eight-way symmetry to create square or rectangular shapes. The default setting is twelve-way symmetry, which produces hexagonal or snowflake shapes.

The Colors menu offers a variety of colors. In this demo version, you get a five-color mode by default. In this mode, Kaleidoscope draws red, green, blue, and white colors on a black background. A wide range of additional colors is available with the registered full version, including an eight-color mode with cyan, magenta, and yellow added to the basic set of five colors. There is also an LCD mode for drawing black on a white background.

behind the trick

This colorful, kaleidoscopic shareware program and screen-saver was written and copyrighted by Clinton Parker. You may distribute unmodified copies of the program freely. However, if you use it or would like a copy that allows you to change the settings, send a check for $10.00 to

Clinton Parker
P.O. Box 3506
Reston, VA 22090

Lava Lamp

.the big picture

The Lava Lamp (LAVA.EXE) is a neat and eye-catching little application that displays pretty pictures using the palette and color cycling under Windows 3.x. Color cycling requires a 256 color video mode. If you don't have it, you just get a static picture.

.running the program

When you run the Lava Lamp program, you see an empty window at first. You have to click once in the main window to see a menu of options before you can start the lava lamp.

■ Lava lamp lunacy—the story continues...

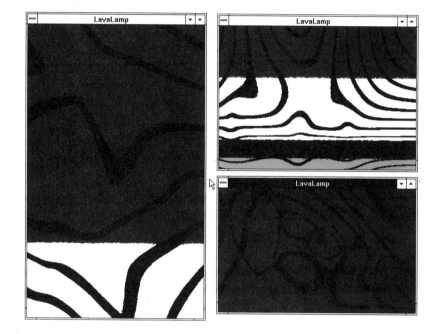

The first choice on the menu is Go!. Select it and the program will begin to draw the equivalent of the popular lava lamp. Colors and forms flow and blend. It looks as though liquids of two or more densities are being heated inside a bottle or lamp. You can alter the colors, forms, and flows by changing some of the settings on the menus. After you've turned on the lava lamp by clicking on Go!, a subsequent click in the main window displays the Stop! choice where Go! used to be. You can make the lava image be still by clicking on Stop!

You can determine how many separate forms appear in your lava lamp. Click on NumCenters and choose one of the eight form numbers in multiples of four from from 4 to 32. The number you choose determines how many pockets of density liquid are simulated.

You can also determine how many colors to use. In the menu, you can specify from 4 to 256 unique colors as the NumColors variable, depending on what your video system can handle. As mentioned above, color cycling requires a 256 color video mode. You will get a static picture if you don't have 256 colors.

You can also influence how many bands of color superimpose themselves on the lava flows. Just choose one of the five unique BandScale values from 1 to 16.

The various controls create different images and fluctuations. By changing one or more values each time you click on Go!, you make the Lava Lamp program generate a completely unique picture each time.

■ ■ ■ ■ ■ ■ ■ ■ ■ ■ ■ ■ ■ ■ ■ **behind the trick**

Lava Lamp is another freeware program, this time from a company called "semi-Bogus Software." They retain the copyright but don't mind how, when, or to whom you distribute copies of Lava Lamp.

Lines

the big picture

The Lines (LINES.EXE) program generates eye-catching graphics. Straight lines create the illusion of animated and curved images.

running the program

Run Lines and you will be treated to a nonstop display of graphical ingenuity. Colored patterns emerge, and attractive geometric figures appear and disappear by the moment. The program creates graphic patterns by drawing straight lines of different lengths and different spacial separations.

◘ Curvilinear art:
You are the artist
and change the
color, separation,
and number of
lines.

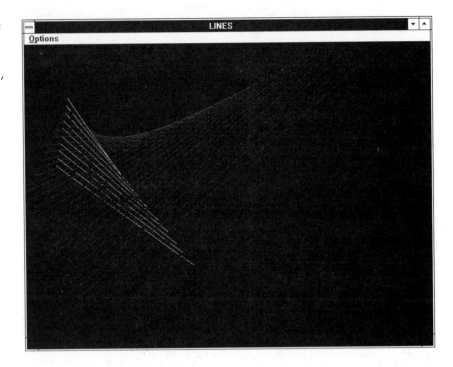

You can influence the images in three ways, each of which is available from the Options menu.

◘ Increase or decrease the solidity of the graphic image by entering a number in the Number of Lines field.

◘ Increase or decrease the density of the image by entering a value for the Maximum Step. This controls the spacing of the lines.

◘ Change the multicolored images to a single color by clicking on the Monochrome check box.

▫ ▫ ▫ ▫ ▫ ▫ ▫ ▫ ▫ ▫ ▫ ▫ ▫ ▫ ▫ ▫behind the trick

Lines was written by Gerald Hogsett of Palo Alto, California. It is freeware. If you like it, he asks you to pass it along to friends and upload it to bulletin boards. I like this particular geometric color display. It is the basis for many screen-saver displays, which I've always enjoyed on my computers.

Mountain Fractal

■ ■ ■ ■ ■ ■ ■ ■ ■ ■ ■ ■ ■ ■ ■ ■ ■ .the big picture

The Mountain Fractal (MOUNFRAC.EXE) program generates a completely new mountainside landscape each time you click on the Fractals option on the main menu.

■ ■ ■ ■ ■ ■ ■ ■ ■ ■ ■ ■ ■ ■ .running the program

Run the program and you will see its full-screen startup window. The main window area is completely black in anticipation of the colorful landscape that will soon appear.

■ Cheaper than a vacation to the mountains and not as tiring as an alpine trek.

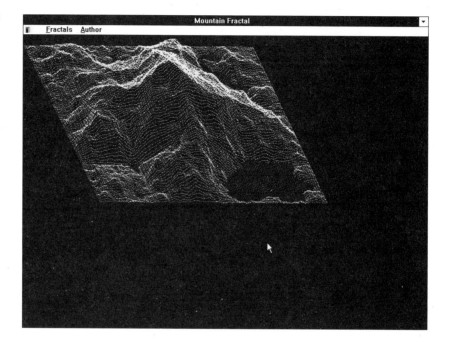

Imagine yourself in an airplane flying over the Rockies or the Adirondacks. Each time you look out the window you see an entirely new vista of hills, valleys, and lakes. That's what happens each time you press Alt-F or click on the Fractals main menu choice in this program.

The program—it's very fast—takes a few seconds to create its vista with fractal geometry. Lush green hills are dotted with small mountain lakes. Shadows give the illusion of depth to the hills and dales in the novel three-dimensional landscape. The size and shape of the geographic landscape change and shift each time you request a new image.

When you tire of these images, close the Mountain Fractal window by clicking on the yellow mini-icon on the left side of the main menu bar.

▫ ▫ ▫ ▫ ▫ ▫ ▫ ▫ ▫ ▫ ▫ ▫ ▫ ▫ ▫ **behind the trick**

I like this program. Click a button and an entirely new landscape forms before your eyes. Unfortunately, the address the author gave in the README.1ST file isn't up to date. But you might try contacting him on his personal bulletin bulletin board:

C.I.F.–B.B.S.
(809) 544-2929
1200/2400/9600/14400HST
24 Hours
Santo Domingo
DOMINICAN REPUBLIC

Messages should be addressed to JiffySoft or Carlos Fragio, who is the SYSOP (SYStem OPerator) of the bulletin board.

Mountain Fractal is a freeware product copyrighted by JiffySoft. It may be distributed for evaluation purposes only. It is not in the public domain, and it is not free software. JiffySoft grants users a license to use this software providing that the program is not modified in any way, including but not limited to decompiling, disassembling, or any other way of reverse-engineering the code.

All users are granted permission to copy Mountain Fractal for distribution to others for evaluation, as long as it is copied in unmodified form. All files, programs, documentation, copyrights and other notices must be copied intact.

No fee or compensation may be charged for the evaluation copy, except to cover the media in which it is distributed, and shipping expenses must be clearly identified as such.

The program may not be used in any unlawful or illegal manner. JiffySoft is in no way responsible for any damages resulting from the use or inability to use Mountain Fractal.

Spirograph

the big picture

The Spirograph (SPIRO.EXE) program is a delightful automated spirograph toy for the computer screen. Watch the constantly changing geometric patterns and shapes being drawn in the multi-colored window.

running the program

Just start the program and watch the entertainment begin. You needn't do anything because the program automatically generates an unending series of colorful patterns and designs.

□ Childlike fun in an adultlike medium.

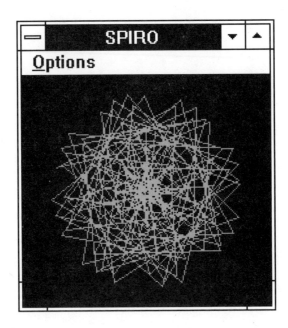

Spirograph creates its patterns by drawing several imaginary circles and averaging the integral points. Before each pattern is actually drawn in the SPIRO window, a random set of values is chosen for each circle's characteristics. You can control these values as well as the number of circles used by the program to create its images.

Pull down the Options menu and select the Preferences choice. You'll see the Spirograph Preferences dialog box. The fields in this box are self-explanatory. You use them for specifying such things as

□ The number of circles to use.

□ Whether or not to use color.

□ Whether a restart request should begin at the coordinate origin.

□ Selection ranges for the geometric characteristics of the circles.

If you manipulate the preferences to a point where you no longer enjoy the images, just push the Restore Default Settings button. Spirograph will reset all settings to their original values.

▫ ▫ ▫ ▫ ▫ ▫ ▫ ▫ ▫ ▫ ▫ ▫ ▫ ▫ ▫ behind the trick

Spirograph was written by Jerry Hogsett of Redwood City, California. It is freeware. He has passed it into the public domain. Although his address is not known, he can be contacted at

CompuServe: 73730,2460

trick 41 ♠

Stars

■ ■ ■ ■ ■ ■ ■ ■ ■ ■ ■ ■ ■ ■ ■ ■ ■ ■ ■.the big picture

The Stars (STARS.EXE) program fills the Windows desktop with stars. The effect is similar to looking through a spaceship window.

■ ■ ■ ■ ■ ■ ■ ■ ■ ■ ■ ■ ■ ■ ■ ■.running the program

When you run the Stars program, the Windows desktop background goes black and small multicolored stars shoot towards your point of view. You also see a small planet icon. In the figure, I moved it to the left side of the screen. Click on this icon to display the System menu and its options.

■ Move your desktop through space at warp speed.

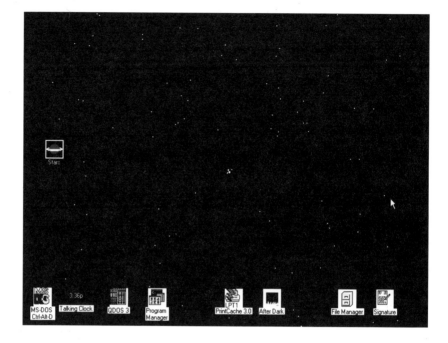

You can make the stars move faster to make it seem as though you're riding a spacecraft at warp speed through outer space. To do this, click on the Warp Speed toggle switch. To slow down your spacecraft, click on the Impulse Drive toggle switch. When you click on one of these two alternatives, the check mark appears beside your new choice instead of the other one.

If you simply want a starry night as your wallpaper, not the moving stars, click on the Stop Engines option on the Stars System menu.

Finally, if you don't want anyone else to be able to fiddle with your starship controls, just click on Hide Icon. No one, including yourself, will be able to make any engine-room control changes to your spacecraft. However, you know one thing that no one else who uses your computer knows: running Stars a second time terminates all previous settings. If you selected Hide Icon from the System menu once, you can rerun Stars the same way you did the first time.

Your second attempt to run it will recognize that the program is running already, and it will automatically shut down the program.

■ ■ ■ ■ ■ ■ ■ ■ ■ ■ ■ ■ ■ ■ ■ ■ **behind the trick**

The Stars program is freeware from David Stafford. Enjoy it! If you like it, let him know, and feel free to distribute his program to others. Please remember, however, to keep the STARS.EXE and STARS.TXT files together. You may contact the author about this program or others he has written at

David Stafford
Kamakura NS
Bldg 4–F
Onaricho 4–16
Kamakura, Kanagawa 248
JAPAN
CompuServe (CIS): 72411,2670 *or* 76666,2542
MCI: DSTAFFORD 361-6512

Termite

■ ■ ■ ■ ■ ■ ■ ■ ■ ■ ■ ■ ■ ■ ■ ■ ■ ■ **the big picture**

The Termite (TERMITE.EXE) program unleashes a multicolored colony of termites. Either the colony grows unchecked in the window, or you make the colony into an icon and watch it eat away the icon while you work.

■ ■ ■ ■ ■ ■ ■ ■ ■ ■ ■ ■ ■ ■ **running the program**

Run the Termite program and it begins immediately, using a DEFAULT.MIT file to simulate a colony of termites. The colony grows and grows and grows in the main Termite window as multicolored pixels simulate new termites.

◘ What's more exciting than an ant farm? Your own termite colony.

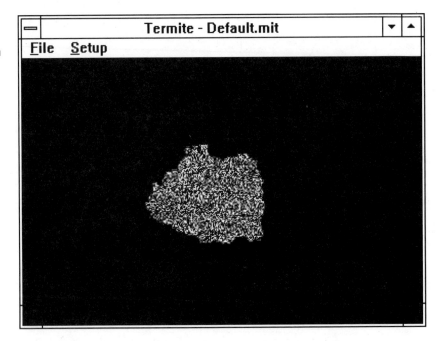

You can throw your own termites into the growing colony by pressing the Ins key on your keyboard. You can also kill termites one at a time by pressing the Del key. However, all pressing Del does is slow the growth down somewhat. Once the colony gets going, killing one or two here and there won't stop the infestation—just like real life.

The Setup menu offers a Pause option if you want to keep the colony at a particular growth level. Or perhaps the color combinations appeal to you or you just want to feel the power of stopping an unstoppable living force. Too bad that real termite infestations aren't this easy to stop.

To simulate what sometimes happens when pest control personnel don't do their jobs right, there is the Restart choice on the Setup menu. Click on it and your termite colony will hatch again and attack the Termite window or its icon.

At first there will be only one termite. Press the Ins key to add new termites to the display or the delete key to remove them. A maximum of 25 termites and a minimum of one are the current limits.

◦ ◦ ◦ ◦ ◦ ◦ ◦ ◦ ◦ ◦ ◦ ◦ ◦ ◦ ◦ ◦ **behind the trick**

This program was written by Hans Kellner, a resident of Scottsdale, Arizona. It is freeware. He released it into the public domain and only asks that you have fun using it and pass it along. He assumes no liability for the program's use, misuse, or disuse.

Winplay

• the big picture

The Winplay (WINPLAY.EXE) program plays polyphonic musical compositions through your PC's speaker.

• • • • • • • • • • • • • • • • running the program

Run Winplay to make the Windows Music Play window appear. To play a sample musical composition, just pull down the Play menu. You'll see the Play dialog box, as shown in the figure. Highlight one of the six sample melodies that come with the package and click on Play. You probably didn't know that a PC speaker could sound so good.

◘ Even if you can't carry a tune, your computer can.

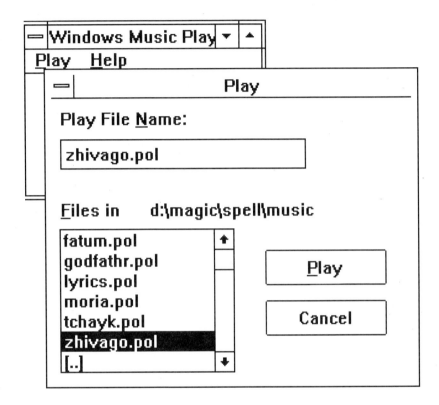

You can also enter the following command line to run a specific melody:

WINPLAY melody-file-name

This will play the pre-recorded melody found in the file specified as the first parameter.

The Introduction of this book explains how to install a program as a selectable icon. One very fun way to use Winplay is to install it in the Program Manager with a separate icon for each different melody. When you choose New Program Item, you would enter WINPLAY *melody-file-name* as the command line, using a different *melody-file-name* for each different icon. Then, you could click on a different icon for each different melody.

■ ■ ■ ■ ■ ■ ■ ■ ■ ■ ■ ■ ■ ■ ■ ■ ■ **behind the trick**

This entertaining musical player program was brought to the freeware world by Sergey Ryzhkov, who lives in Moscow. The only contact information I've been able to find is his e-mail address:

e-mail: sir@hq.demos.su

If anybody knows how to reach Sergey, please write to me and I'll include information about him in the next printing of this book.

Xmas Tree Icon

The Xmas Tree Icon (TREE.EXE) program is the ultimate in Windows dressing: a Christmas tree in icon form with gifts and blinking lights.

■ Decorate your Windows desktop with this animated Christmas tree icon.

■ ■ ■ ■ ■ ■ ■ ■ ■ ■ ■ ■ ■ ■ ■running the program

Start the program and a Christmas tree icon appears complete with trimmings, presents, and blinking lights. You can't open the gifts, but what do you expect? You aren't friends with the program author. Perhaps if you send him a Christmas card his next version will have gift boxes you can open up. Then again, he does make the point that the tree in his living room doesn't do much more than this icon does—it just sits there too.

Since it's just a decoration, the best way to use the program is probably to run it when you start Windows. At least consider doing that during the Thanksgiving to Christmas period when holiday decorations are everywhere. See the Introduction of this book for reminders about how to set up a program for automatic execution. The TREE.EXE program may be found in the XMASICON directory beneath your installed SYBEX directory.

■ ■ ■ ■ ■ ■ ■ ■ ■ ■ ■ ■ ■ ■ ■ behind the trick

This lighthearted program was written by Al Fontes, Jr. It is freeware. He suggests passing it along to anyone you like, and passing along the accompanying text file too. His only wish when he placed this in the public domain was to receive a Christmas card from you. Don't disappoint him. Send the card to

Al Fontes, Jr.
33 Mahogany Drive
San Rafael, CA 94903

Yin Yang

■ ■ ■ ■ ■ ■ ■ ■ ■ ■ ■ ■ ■ ■ ■ ■ ■ ■ ■ **the big picture**

The Yin Yang (YINYANG.EXE) program draws a variation of the familiar T'ai Chi symbol. This symbol is supposed to represent the dual nature of all living things. In fact, if you look closely at the drawing, you'll see a cross between the historic Yin Yang symbol and the modern-day floppy disk.

■ ■ ■ ■ ■ ■ ■ ■ ■ ■ ■ ■ ■ ■ ■ ■ **running the program**

What's to do? Sit at your computer and stare. Curl up on the floor in front of the computer and gaze. Question the wisdom of running

■ Practice Zen
meditation with this.

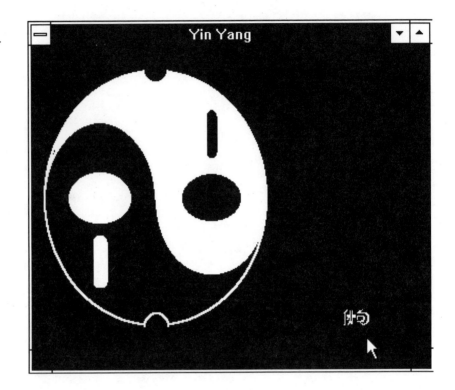

this program, or looking at this image, or questioning what you are
questioning.

behind the trick

James M. Curran invented this program. It is freeware and he asks
no registration fee for it. He also wrote the Horse program that appears elsewhere in this book.

James offers this copyrighted program free to the public in hopes of making everyone's computer a nicer place to visit. You can contact him at

James M. Curran
24 Greendale Road
Cedar Grove, NJ 07009-1313
CompuServe: 72261,655

abracadabra

Okay, you rested in Part III, "Spellbound." While the programs did most of the work, you just sat there and watched. But the programs in this part require you to participate. They will engage and delight you. Some of them are games and challenges that will make you think. All are colorful, and they will entertain and mystify you.

Some of the programs here are functional—the calculator inside an icon, the pin-up notes, and the While You Were Out telephone message center. Every one of them presents itself in such an engaging manner you'll have a hard time suppressing a smile when you use them.

For those of you who just need a fun break from work, there are games here to entertain you. You can challenge yourself with slide and peg puzzles, or with two variations on a game similar to the old favorite, Tetris. You can challenge a friend and play a cannon game, or challenge no one and just use your mouse pointer as a paddle to bounce balls around the screen.

Bandit

▪ ▪ ▪ ▪ ▪ ▪ ▪ ▪ ▪ ▪ ▪ ▪ ▪ ▪ ▪ ▪the big picture

The Bandit (BANDIT.EXE) program works like a slot machine, also known as a "one-armed bandit." When you pull the handle, the three reels spin around and stop at random. Payouts, calculated on the center line, are made according to the chart posted on the machine. To "pull" the handle, press the spacebar, press Alt-P, or click on Play with the mouse. Press F1 for help.

▪ ▪ ▪ ▪ ▪ ▪ ▪ ▪ ▪ ▪ ▪ ▪ ▪ ▪ ▪running the program

The author wrote this program for sheer amusement, and as an exercise to learn the Windows' API. He was very generous. His machine

■ Beating this bandit won't cost you a cent.

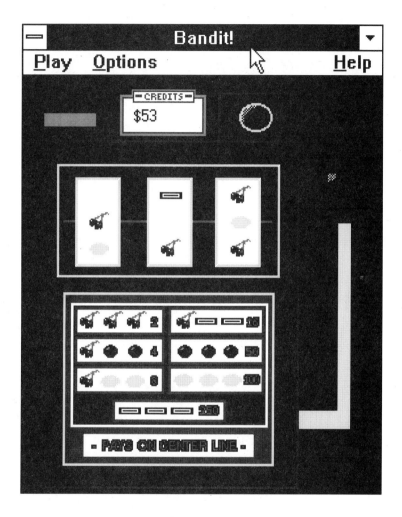

offers an approximate 97 percent payback rate over the long haul. With this kind of programming, you probably don't have to be warned not to use this program for gambling.

This program uses 16 color bitmaps. Consequently, it may not display properly on monochrome or CGA displays. But it is simple, colorful, and produces fun sound effects. If you want to play this in your office, turn off the sound by pulling down the Options menu and selecting the one choice found there.

When you pull the handle, it actually appears to move down, which makes for a nice visual touch. And when the slot machine wheels come up with a winning line, the flag at the top-left of the machine flashes while you are paid off. The game always starts you off with $50.00 and deducts $1.00 for each play, adding money to the Credits window whenever you come up with a winning combination.

▪ ▪ ▪ ▪ ▪ ▪ ▪ ▪ ▪ ▪ ▪ ▪ ▪ ▪ ▪ behind the trick

You may freely distribute the Bandit as long as all files in the SYBEX\BANDIT directory are included. This package is copyrighted by The Wicked Witch Software Company. No fees for the program itself may be charged, although a reasonable copying expense may be charged. Please send any comments to the author at

> The Wicked Witch Software Company
> P.O. Box 3452
> Reno, NV 89505

The author will try to answer all reasonable questions. Naturally, the author does not extend any warranties of any sort. Bandit and its associated documentation is delivered as-is. The user assumes all responsibility for any and all consequences of using this software.

Bang!Bang!

▪ ▪ ▪ ▪ ▪ ▪ ▪ ▪ ▪ ▪ ▪ ▪ ▪ ▪ ▪ ▪ ▪ **the big picture**

The Bang!Bang! (BANGBANG.EXE) program is a cute and easy to play little game. First you see an eye-catching window with two cannons pointed at each other. The object is to adjust the angle of your cannon, and the velocity of your shot, to destroy your opponent's weaponry before he or she does the same to you. Two players alternate shots, although a one-player mode is provided if you just want to improve your aim.

■ It's not golf, but it does take a hole-in-one to win.

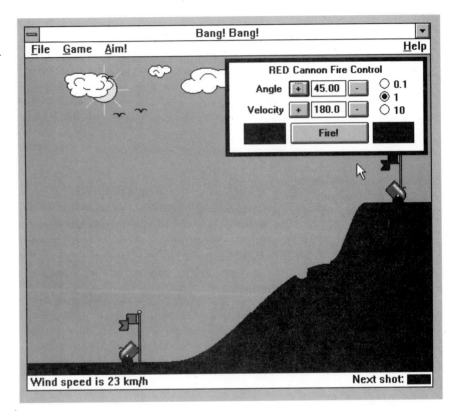

running the program

To begin a game, select New on the Game menu. A new battlefield terrain appears. What the battlefield looks like, the speed and direction of the wind, and the player who gets to shoot first are all randomly determined or selected by the program. You'll know it is your turn when your side's color appears in the Next shot box in the lower-right corner of the window. You can tell which is your color by looking at the flag beside each cannon.

Once a new game is started, the Aim! menu appears, and players may begin firing. If you don't like the terrain, choose the Game/New menu selection until you see a landscape you like.

The object of the game is to destroy the opponent's cannon. To stop a game in progress either choose Stop on the Game menu, or exit the game completely by choosing Exit on the File menu. The Game/Stop option is only available while a game is in progress.

When you choose Stop, the Aim! menu is disabled and you can't fire your cannon anymore. At this point, you can adjust the game's configuration (see below) by choosing Configure on the Game menu, start a new game, or end the program by choosing Exit.

To start firing your cannon, select the Aim! menu. You'll see a dialog box for entering the angle and velocity of the cannonball. You can either type the values directly into the fields on the panel or click on the + or − buttons beside each field to raise or lower the angle and velocity of your shot. Adjust the 0.1, 1, and 10 buttons in the dialog box to set the increments by which the field values change when you click the buttons.

Once you have selected the angle and velocity, press the Fire! button. The cannon fires and the cannonball leaves the screen, strikes the ground, or destroys the other player's cannon. Don't forget to take into account the wind factor when you select the angle and velocity of your shot. Wind drag greatly affects the flight of the cannonball.

The Firing Control dialog box "remembers" your most recent settings to make it a little easier to hone in on your opponent.

Select the Configure option on the Game menu to enable, disable, or modify certain play features of Bang! Bang! In the Configuration dialog box that appears, you can change four items:

- **Hit Accuracy** controls how accurate you must be to destroy a target. The three settings are Medium, Fine and Coarse.

- **Wind**, a check box, enables the random wind generator. Check this box and Bang!Bang! will select a random wind speed velocity for each battle, and the wind will blow in a randomly selected direction. When you disable this check box there is no wind.

◻ **Divots**, a check box, causes cannonballs that miss their targets but strike the ground before they leave the play window to explode. When they explode, they create ground craters. Enabling the Divots check box has the effect of gradually eroding the battlefield terrain, which changes the characteristics of the battle.

◻ **1-Player**, another check box, configures Bang!Bang! for practice mode. Check this box to use one cannon and play the game by yourself.

From time to time, you will come across a combination of terrain shape, wind direction, and wind speed that you like and want to recall later. Likewise, you may want to save a game that is in progress in order to resume and finish it later. Bang!Bang! allows you to save the state of the current game. You save it in a State file that you can recall later. To save a game,

1   Select the Save option on the File menu.

2   Enter the name of the file to which you want to save the game. Bang! Bang! uses the default file extension .SAV, but you can use any extension you want by explicitly specifying it.

Recall and resume a saved game with the File/Open option. You'll see a standard Windows dialog box with a list of files and directories. Enter the name of the State file you want to load (the default extension is .SAV), or select a file name from the list, and press the Open button.

tips and hints

It takes longer to narrow in on your opponent when you vary both the angle and velocity parameters. It is much better to pick an angle or velocity that gets you close to your target, and then vary the other parameter to hone in on it.

Depending on the layout of the battlefield, and the speed and direction of the wind, sometimes your target seems impossible to hit. In some layouts, for example, when there is a high hill between cannons and the wind is blowing hard, neither opponent appears to be able to hit the other.

When a ball leaves either side of the game window, it is considered gone, and the next player's turn comes up. This, however, is not true of the top of the window. When a ball passes through the top of the window, it will reenter the window later on. In this way you can fire over hills.

behind the trick

Bang!Bang! is distributed as shareware, but may be copied and distributed freely, providing that no changes are made to the program. It was inspired by a game called SHOOT that the author, David Lutton, originally encountered on a Tektronix S-3270 ATE (test system). David is pleased with the way his game turned out, and hopes that you agree and enjoy playing it. When you register, send along your name, address, and any comments, hints, or suggestions you have. David will file the information and let you know when a new version is available.

You can contact the author (donate $10.00 to him for his programming efforts) at

David B. Lutton II
R.D. Box 1195
Cambridge, VT 05444

Button Madness

The Button Madness (BTNMAD.EXE) program is a deceptively difficult but entertaining bit of a diversion. The only requirement here is to turn all sixteen squares from green to red. Each time you click on a square, it changes color. Simple, huh? Nope, because when the clicked-on square changes color, so does each one of its North-South-East-West neighbor squares.

A crazy quilt with a checkered past.

running the program

When you first run the program, a window appears with a four-by-four array of green squares. Click on a square and it changes from green to red. The goal is to change the solid pattern of green squares to a solid pattern of red squares.

It seems easy at first. Unfortunately, after a couple of key presses, you discover that the window looks like the figure shown here. Some squares are green and some are red. Each new mouse click turns the clicked-on square a different color, but also changes the color of each adjacent square. It quickly begins to seem hopeless, especially since clicking on an outside square changes the color of the square on the opposite side of the window.

This particular phenomenon is called "wrapping around." Big deal. Knowing what it's called doesn't help one little bit in solving this insidious puzzle. If you don't manage to solve it on your own, turn to the end of this book for the solution.

■ ■ ■ ■ ■ ■ ■ ■ ■ ■ ■ ■ ■ ■ ■ ■ ■ **behind the trick**

I enjoyed this little freeware puzzle, but perhaps only because I figured it out before frustration set in. It was written by David W. Palmer and was based on an idea by Chris E. Allison. You can reach the author at

e-mail: CALLISON@YODA.EECS.WSU.EDU

Columns

■ ■ ■ ■ ■ ■ ■ ■ ■ ■ ■ ■ ■ ■ ■ ■ ■ ■ **.the big picture**

Columns (COLUMNS.EXE) is a very fun and colorful variant of the ever-popular Tetris game. Rather than maneuvering falling blocks to make solid rows, this game consists of falling columns. Each column contains three square blocks of a different color. You must maneuver the falling columns so that the blocks within the falling column position align themselves with blocks that have fallen already. You get a point each time you create an alignment of three or more blocks.

■ A clever variation of the old Tetris standard.

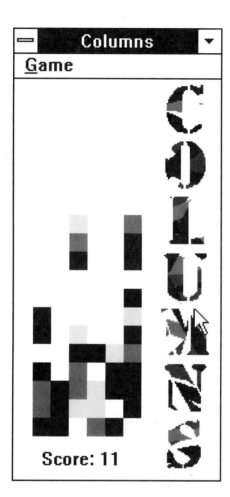

running the program

When you run the program, the Columns window appears and columns begin to fall down the window. Your job is to move the falling columns to the left or right, or cycle the three colors, so that when the column lands it is aligned with three or more blocks of the same color. Three or more blocks aligned in the vertical, horizontal, or diagonal direction is considered a successful alignment.

When three or more blocks are aligned, they disappear. Blocks above the disappearing ones immediately fill in the gap, which creates a new configuration of colored blocks. At this time you receive a point for your alignment. If you align more than one series of blocks at the same time, say in both the vertical and diagonal directions, you receive a separate point for each series. Similarly, if the blocks that fill the gap after a series disappears create a new alignment, you receive an additional point.

You can control the falling columns with your keyboard in several ways:

← or →	moves a falling column to the left or right.
↑	rotates the three colored blocks within a falling column (you can also press the 5 key on the numeric keypad).
↓	drops the column the remaining distance immediately (you can also press 0 on the numeric pad, or the spacebar).
−	halts the game and minimizes the window—an option provided for those of you who plan to play the game on your office computer. (Press the gray minus key at the right side of the numeric keypad, not the minus key on your keyboard.)

Once you get good at maneuvering the colored blocks, try to do better than getting just three in a row, which is only worth a point. Four blocks in a row scores two points, five scores three points, and so on. The configurations that score the most points involve diagonal sequences because the falling blocks that fill the gap create the largest number of new patterns.

The game ends only when the playing field fills up and the new column has nowhere to fall. Unlike some games, no bonuses are given for fast play, so there is no reason to drop the columns quickly.

If you want to see how well you've done (or someone else has done) in preceding games, pull down the Game menu and select the Show High Scores choice.

■ ■ ■ ■ ■ ■ ■ ■ ■ ■ ■ ■ ■ ■ ■ ■ ■ **behind the trick**

This program comes a long way from John Rotenstein, who lives in Australia. He distributes it for free, under what he lightly terms the HappiWare (TM) system:

"If you like it, remember to smile!"

In reality, however, he simply would like to receive a postcard from you, just to see how far his efforts have traveled. You can write him at

John Rotenstein
P.O. Box 165
Double Bay, NSW 2028
AUSTRALIA

When you write, mention "Col 1.1" so he knows which version made it to your area.

E mlith

▪ ▪ ▪ ▪ ▪ ▪ ▪ ▪ ▪ ▪ ▪ ▪ ▪ ▪ ▪ ▪ ▪ ▪ ▪ the big picture

Emlith (EMLITH.EXE) is a colorful variation of the now famous Tetris game. This Windows version, written by Yutaka Emura, requires you to maneuver falling objects, called "liths," to form solid rows. When a row is filled with squares your score increases, the row is removed from the screen, and new liths fall into the available space to merge with already fallen liths. The more space you open up, the more time you have to move or rotate the falling liths into a better position.

■ An original Tetris clone, with imaginative optional variations.

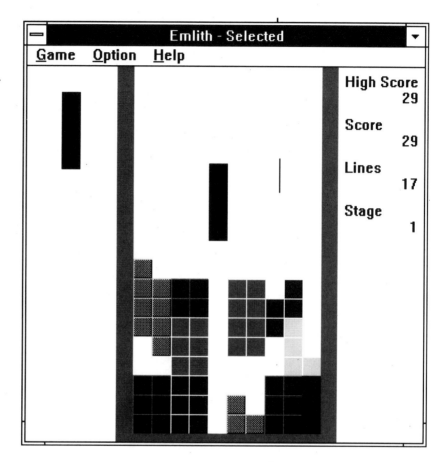

running the program

Start the program any way you choose and the game will begin immediately. A falling lith consists of four squares connected to each other—the default and traditional size of a falling object in the original Tetris game.

You can control the falling liths with either your keyboard or the mouse. Click the left mouse button on the falling lith to rotate it. Click to the right or the left of the lith to move it from side to side. Use the right mouse button to drop the lith into place.

The following keys on the numeric keypad control the position of the falling liths:

6 *or* →	moves the lith to the right
4 *or* ←	moves the lith to the left
8 *or* ↑	moves the lith down
2 *or* ↓	drops the lith
5	rotates the lith
Esc	halts the game

You can change the function of the ↑ and ↓ keys as well as the spacebar. To do so, select the Assign Keys menu option.

When you fill in an entire row, it disappears and you earn one point. The more rows you complete at the same time, the more points you earn. Here is how scoring works:

1 row = 1 point

2 rows = 5 points

3 rows = 10 points

4 rows = 20 points

5 rows = 50 points

6 rows = 100 points

The best way to play Emlith is to create solid rows but leave a single column in the middle or on the side. This way, when a vertical lith appears, you can complete multiple rows easily. Maneuvering a 4 × 1 lith into a vertical gap completes four rows and earns 20 points at once.

game menu commands

The Game menu offers basic choices for running Emlith.

- **New** starts the game again. A blank screen appears and there is no score.

- **Pause** suspends the game so you can switch to another system task without losing your position in the game.

- **Resume** continues a suspended game.

- **Stage Forward** advances the game to the next stage in challenge mode.

- **Stage Backward** returns you to the previous stage in Challenge mode.

- **Exit** lets you quit the Emlith game.

option menu commands

Emlith has an Option menu for changing the configuration defaults of the game. Choose Play Mode on this menu and a dialog box appears. In this box you can choose the number of squares in the falling liths, as well as how much the pattern of each lith varies.

The second major choice on the Options menu is Frame Width. With this option you can change the width of your playing area, except in Challenge mode. When the Frame Width dialog box appears, enter a number in the field to tell the program how many blocks should constitute a row.

Choose Assign Keys to change the functionality of the ↑ key, ↓ key, or the spacebar. Click on the Drop, Rotate, or Down button to assign a new functionality to the key.

Choose Settings on the Options menu and Emlith will open up a dialog box with a miscellany of controls. In the Background section, you can control the background color of the playing area by clicking on System (the default), White, or Black. Choose Vertical Lines if you need help seeing where a lith will fall if you drop it from high in the playing area. A series of parallel vertical lines will appear as guides so you can see the falling path of each lith. Choose Monochrome to set the game colors for use on a monochrome monitor. Select Save Size before you exit if you want to retain both the game size and the location of the game window when you exit the game. Finally, the Default Size choice on the Options menu restores the window to its default size, which is ten blocks per row.

▪ ▪ ▪ ▪ ▪ ▪ ▪ ▪ ▪ ▪ ▪ ▪ ▪ ▪ ▪ behind the trick

Emlith is shareware, and Yutaka says that the trial period for this game is one week. If you decide to continue playing the game after this period, please register your copy. After you register, you will be able to choose the starting stage in Challenge mode and the registration request will stop appearing.

You can register your version of Emlith in two ways, each of which is explained in REGE.TXT file in the \SYBEX\EMLITH directory. In any event, if you have questions, suggestions, or wish to register, you may reach the author at

> Yutaka Emura
> 920-1, Higashihiratsuka,
> Tsukuba, Ibaraki 305
> JAPAN
> CompuServe: 73560,2250

Although the copyright of this application belongs to Yutaka Emura, you can freely copy and distribute his programs for non-commercial purposes.

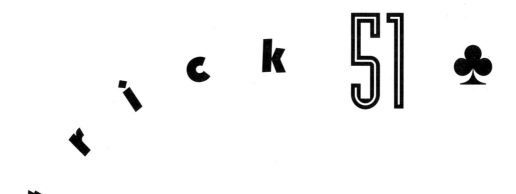

Fences

• • • • • • • • • • • • • • • • the big picture

Fences (FENCES.EXE) is a game for two players. Each player takes turns connecting pairs of dots in an attempt to build a fence from one side of the board to the other.

• • • • • • • • • • • • • running the program

Run the Fences program and the window shown in the figure appears. Lines don't appear until you begin playing, and the initial size of the playing field is seven by seven dots, the Small Board size. One player connects red dots and the other player builds a fence by connecting blue dots. You can choose among three

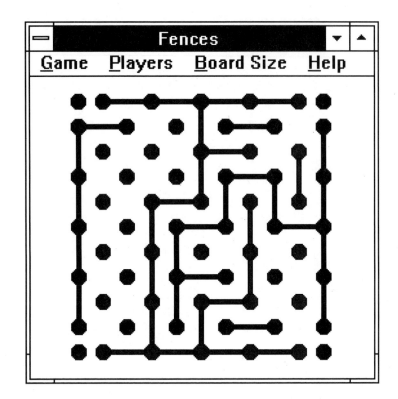

playing-area sizes. Pull down the Board Size menu and choose Small Board for a seven by seven grid, Medium Board for a more challenging nine by nine grid, or Large Board for a thirteen by thirteen grid. But don't venture onto the Large Board until you've improved to the point of winning frequently at the smaller board sizes. You can beat the computer at any size grid, although you'll have to concentrate. It's not a cinch, by any means.

The Players menu offers four choices. You can set the game up for two human players, for one human and the computer, or for the computer to play against itself. Most importantly, you can define the skill level of the computer from the Players menu by choosing among the three skill levels—Good, Better, and Best—for both the Red and the Blue player. Even the Good level is a challenge for the computer. Good is the default and you should only advance beyond it when you've learned the game well enough to beat the computer often at the Good level.

After you've won a game (as shown in the figure), the complete fences stay on-screen so you can admire them. When you're ready to begin a new game, just press F2 or pull down the Game menu and select New. On the Game menu is an Exit choice for removing the Fences window from your desktop.

To connect two dots, position the mouse pointer between the dots and click once. The line is drawn. If you're playing against the computer, its line will appear almost instantly after yours, and so your turn comes up again. The Red player always gets to play first. By default, the human player uses the red dots, but you can change this setting from the Players menu if you get really cocky about your skills.

You cannot connect dots through a connection that your opponent has already made. The game ends when one of the players builds a complete fence from one side of the board to the other.

□ □ □ □ □ □ □ □ □ □ □ □ □ □ **behind the trick**

Obviously, the author is not making a big deal about his freeware game. His name is Steve Blanding, but he offers no contact information. Too bad. I like this effort. Nice work, Steve.

Happy Fun Ball

▪ ▪ ▪ ▪ ▪ ▪ ▪ ▪ ▪ ▪ ▪ ▪ ▪ ▪ ▪ ▪ ▪ .the big picture

The Happy Fun Ball (HFBALL.EXE) program bounces a ball around the window frame. The ball is pulled down by gravity, and is slowed by friction when it touches a window border. You can click the mouse inside the window border to give the ball an effective push or pull. The force of the pull increases as the mouse gets farther from the ball.

▪ ▪ ▪ ▪ ▪ ▪ ▪ ▪ ▪ ▪ ▪ ▪ ▪ ▪ .running the program

Run the program and the Happy Fun Ball window opens up. A black ball begins to bounce around on a green background. With

◘ Follow (and lead) the bouncing ball.

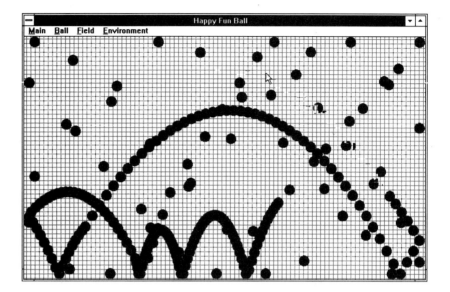

the four menus, you can have as much fun as you like bouncing the ball. You can control its speed, size, and color. You can also implement a number of physical phenomena that influence motion, such as gravity, friction, and directional forces.

The Main menu provides three self-evident choices. Select Reset to return all program variables to their default settings. About shows the standard copyright and authorship information. Exit ends the program.

The Ball menu offers several options that apply specifically to the bouncing ball.

- ◘ **Size** lets you choose a small, medium, or large ball.

- ◘ **Speed** lets you choose a slow, medium, fast, or turbo—really fast—ball movement.

- ◘ **Color** changes the ball's default color from black to either red, green, blue, or white.

❑ **Leave Trail**, my personal favorite, leaves a trail of colored balls on the screen when the main ball moves. As you can see in the figure, I've turned this option on for my system.

The Field menu offers two primary choices, each of which leads to a secondary set of choices. Here you choose a pattern for the background of the window.

The Environment menu offers the unusual opportunity to influence gravity and friction. When you choose Gravity, you see a submenu with five choices: no gravitational force, or else a weak, medium, strong, or reverse force. The first four are self-explanatory; the fifth can be the most fun, since it causes the ball to be pushed up rather than pulled down.

The Default choice on the Environment menu resets both the gravity and friction settings to their weak values.

■ ■ ■ ■ ■ ■ ■ ■ ■ ■ ■ ■ ■ ■ ■ ■ **behind the trick**

Happy Fun Ball (TM), a freeware program, was written and copyrighted by Bert Poston. Bert asks that you send $1000.00 (he's probably kidding!) if you like Happy Fun Ball to

Durbin Development, Inc.
2351 College Station Road
Suite 482
Athens, Georgia 30605
Attn: Bert Poston
e-mail: Poston@Athena.CS.UGA.EDU

Bert's legal disclaimer is fun to read all by itself. Consider it an integral part of this entertaining program. Be sure to read it in the text file that accompanies the program.

Icon Calculator

the big picture

The IconCalc (ICONCALC.EXE) program is a full-function calculator in an icon.

running the program

This is one of those gee-whiz products. When you run the program, a calculator appears in an icon at the bottom of your screen. You can keep it in front of other applications at all times to see it and use it while you work. It takes up very little memory, has context-sensitive help, and offers a variety of color schemes from which to

■ A real calcu-
lator for those with
steady hands and
a keen eye.

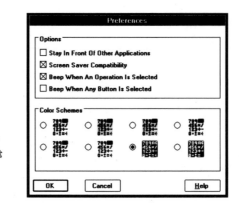

choose. Being able to choose color schemes makes it easier to see all the miniaturized numbers and operators on the icon.

You must use the right mouse button (!) to select buttons on the minicalculator. The left mouse button, as always, is interpreted by Windows and will bring up IconCalc's System menu. You may also use the numbers on the keyboard or the numeric keypad to enter numbers. Remember to toggle the NumLock switch before using the numeric keypad.

To move IconCalc to a more desirable site on your desktop, just click on the IconCalc icon. Then, as you hold the mouse button down, move IconCalc to its new location.

To remove the Icon Calculator from your desktop, just click once on the IconCalc icon. This brings up the System Menu. From there you can click on the Close choice to end the IconCalc task.

The principal choice on the IconCalc System Menu is named Preferences. Click on this option to bring up the Preferences dialog box, as seen in the figure above. In the figure, the icon calculator can be seen just above the mouse pointer and to the left of the Preferences dialog box.

If you place an *X* in the check box labelled Stay In Front Of Other Applications, IconCalc will stay in front of all other application windows on your desktop. You'll be able to see IconCalc in front of an application even if it sends output to the part of the screen where the IconCalc icon is.

Select Screen Saver Compatibility to hide IconCalc when a screen-saver becomes active. IconCalc will reappear after the screen-saver relinquishes control—that is, after you use the keyboard or move the mouse.

To have IconCalc beep when you select a mathematical operation, mark the check box labeled Beep When An Operation Is Selected. Finally, if you want IconCalc to beep when a button on its face is selected, place an *X* in the check box labeled Beep When Any Button Is Selected.

IconCalc can display exponents. IconCalc will display "Error" if you attempt to divide a number by zero. Click on "AC" or press the letter *C* on the keyboard to clear the error.

behind the trick

The author welcomes your comments and suggestions, as well as reports of any problems. You can contact him at

> David A. Feinleib
> 1430 Massachusetts Avenue
> Suite 306-42
> Cambridge, MA 02138
> BIX mail: "pgm"
> CompuServe: 76516,20
> BBS via FIDONET (IBM UG BBS, Boston MA.): Node: 1:101/310 David Feinleib

IconCalc is shareware. You may make copies of this program and give them to others as long as the documentation is provided with the program. Please see the REGISTER.DOC file or read the information in the About box for information about how to register. The registration fee is $12.00 per copy plus shipping and handling. Please include your name, address, and current version number. The version number may be found in the About Box.

Site licenses, LAN licenses, and substantial quantity discounts are available. Customization of IconCalc is available but is not included in the ShareWare registration fee. The fee charged for customization depends on the amount and significance of the customization. Please contact David directly for more information regarding these possibilities.

IconCalc is supplied as-is. The author disclaims all warranties expressed or implied, including, without limitation, the warranties of merchantability and of fitness for any purpose. The author assumes no liability for damages, direct or consequential, which may result from the use of IconCalc.

Peg Puzzle

the big picture

The Peg Puzzle (PEGPUZL.EXE) program presents a peg-jumping
puzzle that the author used to play at his grandmother's house. The
idea of the game is to jump pegs over one another until only one
peg remains.

running the program

Run the program and you see the window above, but with all fifteen pegs in place. You may have seen puzzles similar to this one,
but with different board configurations. I have a wooden puzzle

■ Jump a peg. Remove a peg. Eliminate as many as you can.

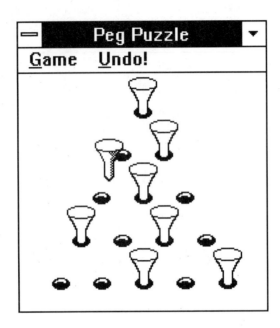

that has marbles instead of pegs and is called Hi-Q. This particular version has 15 holes arranged in the shape of an equilateral triangle.

To legally move a peg you must jump it over another peg into an empty hole. This is also the only way to legally remove a peg. The program requires a two-button mouse—no keyboard interface is provided.

To begin the game, place the mouse pointer on top of a peg and click the right button. The program removes the peg and the game begins. Now move the mouse pointer onto another peg and attempt to drag it with the left mouse button over a neighbor peg and into the empty hole. The jumped-over peg is removed. Continue this procedure until only one peg remains. An Undo option is provided because the author had an Undo option when he was a boy: he'd work himself into a corner, put a few pegs back, and try a different tack until he solved the puzzle.

If you attempt an illegal move, the peg you tried to move is placed back in its starting hole and the computer beeps. By clicking on the

Undo! choice, you can make the program step backward one move at a time.

behind the trick

The author of this shareware program can be reached at

Oscar Waddell
c/o Karen Stillhammer
P.O. Box 132
Hanover, Indiana 47243

The author would like $1.00 for his efforts. In addition, if you would like to receive the DOS program that solves the puzzle in any starting configuration, send him a blank disk and $5.00 with a request for the DOS program.

Pinup Notes

the big picture

The PinUp Notes program (PINUP10.EXE) provides small pop-up windows for taking notes and capturing graphics.

running the program

When you first run the program, a PinUp Notes icon appears at the bottom of your screen. Double-click the left mouse button on the icon to create a text note. Double-click the right mouse button to create a bitmap note. You can create both types of note from the icon's System menu as well.

■ Save a tree. Use these Post-It notes.

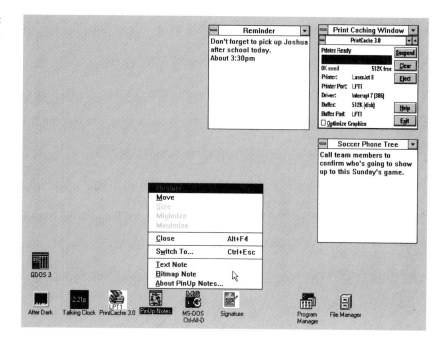

Use text notes to enter and store text from the keyboard. Simply select the note and start typing. Use bitmap notes to copy and store regions of the screen. To do this, select the Grab option from the bitmap note's System menu, and use the mouse to outline the rectangular region you want to copy. The program stretches the image to make it fit in the dimensions of the note window.

You can maximize both kinds of notes. Also, you can change a note's caption to reflect its contents by selecting the Caption option from the note's System menu. Notice in the figure above that I've done that with the three pin-up notes that I created.

When you exit Windows, any notes that are still open are saved in a file named PINUP10.NTS. Notes are restored automatically the next time you start the PinUp Notes program. Loading PinUp Notes when you first start Windows makes this feature particularly useful.

Here's a tip for using Pinup Notes more effectively: click once on the PinUp Notes icon to bring all the pin-up notes to the top of the window being displayed on the screen.

□ □ □ □ □ □ □ □ □ □ □ □ □ □ □ **behind the trick**

PinUp Notes is a shareware program. You are welcome to try it out free of charge, but if you like it and decide to keep it on your system, you are obligated to register your copy by paying $5.95 to the author at the address given below. Registration entitles you to legally use this and all future releases of PinUp Notes, notification of future releases, and limited technical support.

PinUp Notes is provided as-is, without warranty of any kind, either express or implied. No liability is assumed from any damage or loss resulting from the use of this program. You are free to copy and share PinUp Notes with others, as long as the PINUP10.EXE and PINUP10.TXT files are distributed together and are not modified in any way.

Shareware distributors are permitted to include PinUp Notes with their distributions, but any fee charged by the distributor does not cover the $5.95 registration fee that you as the user owe to the author if you decide to keep and use PinUp Notes.

To register your copy of PinUp Notes, send a check or money order for $5.95 to

> Jonathan Reed
> 1575 Agnes Avenue
> Palm Bay, FL 32909
> Internet: jreed@jaguar.ess.harris.com
> Prodigy: rdts35a

Be sure to include your name, full mailing address, and the type of computer on which you are running PinUp Notes.

Reverse Polish Calculator

∎ ∎ ∎ ∎ ∎ ∎ ∎ ∎ ∎ ∎ ∎ ∎ ∎ ∎ ∎ ∎ ∎ ∎ **the big picture**

The Reverse Polish Calculator (RCALC.EXE), or RPN calculator, is a unique tool. Many scientists, engineers, and computer specialists will recognize the different logic it employs.

∎ ∎ ∎ ∎ ∎ ∎ ∎ ∎ ∎ ∎ ∎ ∎ ∎ ∎ **running the program**

RPN calculators require you to enter numbers before the operation is performed. This is very unlike standard calculators, with which

■ A special calculator for HP fans and computerniks.

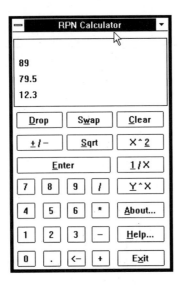

you compute by entering the operators between the numbers you want them to operate on. It took me quite a while to get used to RPN calculators when I first learned to use them in my computer classes.

In RPN, operations have no priority; they are performed in the order entered. Consequently, RPN calculators do not require you to use parentheses. Instead, RPN calculators store numbers on what is called a stack. A "stack" is no more than a pile of entries, much like a stack of dishes. When you enter operators later, such as multiply or divide, the numeric entries on the stack are removed and operated on by the operators one at a time.

understanding the display screen

The stack can hold up to 1024 numbers, but only the top 4 numbers are displayed. Like most RPN calculators, RPN displays the stack upside-down. In other words, the number on the top of the stack is on the bottom of the display.

To make RCALC easier to use, you can press RCALC's buttons in several different ways. Obviously, all buttons can be selected with the mouse. Digits, Enter, +, −, *, /, and the decimal point (.) can be typed from the keyboard or the numeric keypad. If you use the numeric keypad, make sure that the Num Lock light is on. Press the Backspace key to enter the <- calculator button. Help can also be activated by typing F1.

Notice the underlined characters on the Calculator. Select a button by holding down the Alt key and typing the underlined character. For example, you can enter Drop by holding down the Alt key and typing *D*.

The following table briefly summarizes all of RCALC's buttons. In the table, *X* represents the number on the top of the stack—in other words, the last number entered or computed. *Y* represents the previous number located right below *X* on the stack.

Button	Function
Drop	Deletes X.
Swap	Exchanges Y and X.
Clear	Deletes all the numbers on the stack.
+/−	Changes the sign of X.
Sqrt	Gives the square root of X.
X^2	Gives the square of X.
Enter	Places the number just entered on top of the stack, or duplicates the number on top of the stack.
1/X	Gives the reciprocal of X.
Y^X	Gives Y raised to power X.
About...	Gives information about the program.
Help...	Gives on-line help.
Exit	Quits the program.

Button	Function
/	Gives Y divided by X.
*	Gives Y times X.
–	Gives Y minus X.
+	Gives Y plus X.
<-	Deletes the last number character typed.
Ctrl-Insert	Copies X into the Clipboard so that it can be pasted into another program.
Shift-Insert	Puts the number in the Clipboard on top of the stack.

◾ ◾ ◾ ◾ ◾ ◾ ◾ ◾ ◾ ◾ ◾ ◾ ◾ ◾ **behind the trick**

This Reverse Polish Notation program (RCALC) may be freely copied without cost, provided it is not changed in any way. This program is copyrighted shareware by Eric Bergman-Terrell. If you find the program useful, please send $5.00 to

Pocket-Sized Software
8547 East Arapahoe Road
Suite J-147
Greenwood Village, CO 80112

Slide Puzzle

the big picture

Puzzle-8 (SLIDEPUZ.EXE) for Windows is a computerized version of the well-known 8-tile puzzle. You must slide the tiles, one by one, into the correct numeric arrangement.

running the program

To solve the puzzle, you start with a scrambled tile arrangement and move tiles onto the empty square until they are arranged in numeric order with one, two, and three on the top; four, a blank space, and five in the middle; and six, seven, and eight on the bottom row.

■ Challenge yourself to solve this puzzle in the fewest possible moves.

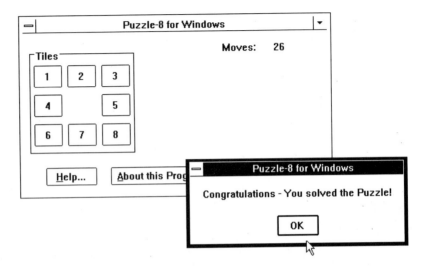

When you start the program, the tiles are scrambled. You have to move one tile at a time into the empty space. Slide a tile one position up, down, left, or right to place it into an empty square. To move a tile, just click on it it with the mouse. The program will beep if you attempt an illegal move. When you're finished running the program, select the Exit Program button.

behind the trick

The Slide Puzzle program is freeware. It may be freely copied without cost, provided it is not changed in any way. If you find the program useful, please send $5.00 to

Pocket-Sized Software
8547 East Arapahoe Road
Suite J-147
Greenwood Village, CO 80112

t r i c k 58 ♥

S tatline

Statline (STAT.EXE) is a small utility program that offers both information and control in a single, sizable screen line. You can jazz it up by configuring it to play pre-recorded music on the hour. Statline displays the mode, day, date, time, and amount of free memory. With Statline, you can launch other Windows applications, keep a small notepad, exit Windows quickly, and delete files. You can even create and call up a menu of your five favorite programs.

■ Not just your current system status. Click on the mini-icons for extra time-saving utility features.

```
┌─────────────────────── Configure Statline ───────────────────────┐
│ ┌─ Mode/Percent ──────────────────┐  ┌─ General Options ──────────────┐
│ │ ◉ Show Percentage of System Resources free │ ☒ Prompt before exiting Windows
│ │ ○ Show Windows Mode              │  ☒ Confirm file deletions
│ └─────────────────────────────────┘  ☐ Keep Statline's window visible
│ ┌─ Memory Display ────────────────┐  ☐ Keep Quick Menu open after run
│ │ ◉ Numeric memory display        │  ☐ Start in "Shortline" mode
│ │ ○ Graphic memory display        │  ☐ Load Progman (if Statline is shell)
│ └─────────────────────────────────┘
│ ┌─ Time Display ──┐ ┌─ Bar Size ─┐   ┌[Unregistered]────────────────┐
│ │ ◉ AM/PM         │ │ ○ Normal   │   License Information
│ │ ○ Day/Night Icons│ │ ◉ Large   │   ┌notepad.exe──────────────────┐
│ └─────────────────┘ └────────────┘   Text Editor
│ ┌─ Chime ─────────────────────────┐  ┌─────────────────────────────┐
│ │ ☒ Chime on the hour             │  Quick Run's initial directory
│ │   ◉ Regular chime    Statline ® ™│
│ │   ○ Play "Asterisk" sound       │          Statline version 3.0
│ │ ☒ Caption Messages   See ORDER.FRM│ (C) Copyright 1991,1992 James Bell
│ │ ┌ Install (first time only) ┐  or HELP for how
│ └─────────────────────────────┘  to register.
│ ┌──────────────── Save Configuration ────────────────┐
└───────────────────────────────────────────────────────┘

75%  Fri Apr 17 9:25 a     15.88 megs ? ◪ ⚡ ▤  EXIT
```

running the program

Run Statline and you'll see a status and control line like the ones in the bottom part of the figure. The top part of the figure shows the Configure Statline dialog box, which you can bring up whenever you like by double-clicking on the Statline display line itself. You can move the dialog box, enlarge it to make it easier to read, or reduce it in size so it takes up less space on your desktop.

Statline is designed to be light on your resources. Usually it uses only a percentage point or two. The display is updated every 12 seconds. In fact, you'll appreciate this fact: Statline performs a Global Compact to reclaim unused memory every 60 seconds. Experienced Windows users can probably just skim this chapter and learn most of Statline's features in just a few moments with the author's on-line Help information.

You can even use Statline instead of the Program Manager as your Windows shell. If you run only a few applications, this technique can save quite a bit of your system resources. To run STATLINE.EXE instead of PROGMAN.EXE as your Windows shell program, you have to edit the SYSTEM.INI file, which is located in the WINDOWS directory. Find the Shell= line in the [Boot] section and change it to

Shell=Statline.exe

You should also copy all the files in the SYBEX\STATLINE directory to your WINDOWS directory. Later on, if you want to let the Program Manager have control of your system again, just use a text editor to change the SYSTEM.INI file back to its original form. You should have made a backup copy (SYSTEM.BAK) prior to making Statline your Windows shell. If you didn't, just change the Shell= line back to what it usually is:

Shell=Progman.exe

and restart Windows.

However, if you make Statline a replacement Windows shell, items found on the Load= or Run= lines in WIN.INI will not actually be loaded when Windows starts. Naturally, if you have Windows 3.1, programs found in the Program Manager's Startup group can't run either.

As you'll learn below, you can configure Statline to display the current Windows mode instead of the percentage of free system resources. Look at the figure: Statline usually displays the day of the week, the date, and the time.

Statline comes with an hourly chime you can turn off and on from the Configure Statline dialog box. The amount of free memory appears to the right of the time of day. In 386 Enhanced mode, this number represents virtual memory, which includes both physical memory and your swapping file size.

If you like, Statline will display a bar graph that shows you the amount of memory being used. Just click on the button beside Graphic Memory Display in the Statline dialog box. You'll see a red bar that grows or shrinks as memory continues to be used on your system. The bar represents the amount of memory consumed or returned to the system since the moment you started Statline. The Statline display is updated every 12 seconds, or when you click the left mouse button on the display area.

the statline display buttons

The left half of the Statline display consists of informational, or status, data. As you know, you can view system mode, memory availability, and so on. On the right side of the Statline display are five mini-icons. Click on one of them to activate a special-purpose utility operation.

In fact, James Bell, the author of the program, has packed extra functionality into these mini-icons in a unique way. Clicking on an icon with the right or left mouse button produces a different result. Learning which button to click does require a slightly higher learning curve, but you can use the Help display to see a brief but very graphic on-line description of what the left and right mouse buttons do. The figure clearly shows a good deal of information packed into a single screen.

the system box

The question mark (?) icon serves two purposes. Click on it with the right mouse button to shrink the Statline display. Statline will remove some of the information, in particular the day/date information. The three mini-icons in the middle of the five are taken off as well. A double-headed arrow icon, the Restore icon, replaces the question mark. Click on the Restore icon at any time to restore the original Statline display.

☐ Help is always just a key-press or a mouse-click away.

Statline Help		
The Ultimate Windows Status Line		
🖱 *Left Button*		🖱 *Right Button*
The System Box F1 Configure and adjust Statline's display.	❓	**Shorten Statline's** F6 display.
MiniPad F2 A tiny notepad; can cut and paste with the Clipboard.	✏️	**Launch text** F7 editor.
Quick Run F3 Launch Windows programs or DOS; Edit/delete files.	🏃	**Open a DOS** F8 Window.
Quick Menu F4 Keep a menu of up to seven often-used programs.	▤	**Bring up Program** F9 Manager
Quick Exit F5 Exit Windows	EXIT	**Exit, then restart** Windows.

OK

🗒   🏃   **S**tatli**n**E   ▤   EXIT
              Version 3.0
James Bell   4511 Sherwood Trace   Gainesville, FL 32605
Phone: (904) 372-3695   Internet: jb1@cis.ufl.edu
Statline is part of a growing number of Windows Utilities, you can register for as little as $10, please see ORDER.FRM for how to order. Checks or money orders in US dollars please.

Click on the question mark icon with the left mouse button to bring up Statline's System menu. Its six buttons provide you access to the following facilities:

- ☐ **Configure** configures Statline.

- ☐ **Arrange Icons** arranges your desktop's icons.

- ☐ **Exit Statline** closes the Statline window.

- ☐ **Move Window** moves Statline's default position.

- ☐ **Cancel** does nothing. The Statline display is restored.

- ☐ **Help** displays a separate Help screen.

the minipad

The second mini-icon from the left looks like a mini flip pad; it symbolizes text editing. Press F2 or click on this icon with the left mouse button and you will see a small (about 700 characters) notepad for writing quick notes to yourself. Notice the buttons in the Minipad window. You can cut and copy to the Windows clipboard, as well as paste from it. The contents of the Minipad are not saved when you exit Windows.

Press F7 or click on the mini flip pad icon with the right mouse button to make Statline launch a program. I know it says "text editor" in the Help screen, but don't let that fool you. By default, Statline runs the program whose name appears in the Text Editor field of the Configure Statline dialog box.

quick run

The mini-icon in the middle is called the Quick Run box. Click on this icon with the right mouse button to start a DOS command session from within Windows. Click on it with the left mouse button to make the Quick Run dialog box appear. From this box, you can run any Windows application quickly simply by double-clicking on its .EXE filename.

You can also launch a DOS session by clicking on the DOS Window button. To delete a file, highlight a file name by clicking on it in this dialog box, and choose the Delete File button. In the same fashion, you can edit a text file by clicking first on the file name and next on the Edit File button.

quick menu

Click on the fourth mini-icon with the left mouse button and Statline will display a menu with seven command lines. If a program name appears on one of the lines, you only need to click on the Run button next to that line to make the program run. Statline will launch that application immediately. You can also select the Run All button to launch all seven—or however many are filled in—programs at once.

To edit command entry lines in this dialog box, just click on one of the entry field boxes and type a valid path, such as C:\WIN-DOWS\WINWORD\WINWORD.EXE. If the program is in your Windows directory or on the DOS PATH, you only need to type in the program name—for example, CARDFILE.

When you select Close, or you click on any of the Run options to execute programs, all of the current command lines are saved for future display and use.

Click on the Quick Menu icon with the right mouse button or press F9 to access a unique feature of Statline. Obviously, you will want the Program Manager around most of the time, but you can save system resources in a special way. Make Statline your usual system shell and run the PROGMAN.EXE program when you want access to the Program Manager's capabilities. In this way, you reduce the usual burden on Windows resources by running a less demanding shell. However, if you need a Program Manager facility, just press F9 or click with the right mouse button to open the Program Manager.

Later, when you're done with the Program Manager, which is now acting just like any other application program, you can close it without exiting Windows. This option has no apparent effect if Statline is not the Windows shell.

To make installing Statline even easier, the Configure dialog box offers a special Install button. Do not click on it now, unless you wish to incorporate Statline in your system in some automatic way. The Install button is located near the lower-left corner of the dialog box. Click on this button and you will see two choices. You can have Statline install itself as the Windows shell, or simply force Statline to load itself the next time you start Windows.

After you click on Install, Statline displays its special Installing Statline dialog box. If you choose No here, STAT.EXE will put itself on the LOAD= line in the WIN.INI file. Answer No if you want Statline to load automatically each time you start Windows.

Choose Yes and STAT.EXE will replace whatever is on the SHELL= line of the SYSTEM.INI file. Answer Yes if you want to be able to save resources, still use the Program Manager on demand, and be able to close the Program Manager later on without leaving Windows.

the exit alternatives

Click on the Exit icon with the left mouse button to quit Windows immediately. By default, you will be prompted before you exit, but this feature can be turned off. To do so, clear the first check box, called Prompt before exiting Windows, in the General Options section of the Configure Statline dialog box.

If for some reason you want to exit Windows and restart Windows immediately, you can also do that. Just click on the Exit icon with the right mouse button. You might have made changes to your WIN.INI or SYSTEM.INI files that require you to restart Windows for the changes to take effect. If that is the case, this option will save you a small amount of time.

▫ ▫ ▫ ▫ ▫ ▫ ▫ ▫ ▫ ▫ ▫ ▫ ▫ ▫ ▫ ▫ ▫.behind the trick

Statline was written and copyrighted by James Bell. You can register your shareware version with him or contact him for any other reason at

> James Bell
> 4511 Sherwood Trace
> Gainesville, FL 32605
> (904) 372-3695
> Internet: jb1@cis.ufl.edu
> The Looking Glass BBS-9600-1200 baud, 8N1, 24 Hours
> (904) 332-2954

James offers two ways in which to register his program. For $10.00, he'll send you a license number that enables you to remove the occasional registration reminder notice that pops up. For $15.00, he'll send you the latest version of Statline. Print out the ORDER.FRM file in the SYBEX\STATLINE directory for all the details. Please be sure to include an extra $2.00 for postage if you live outside the US. And be sure your check or money-order is in US dollars.

WinPong

.the big picture

The WinPong (WINPONG.EXE) program displays a little ball that bounces around your screen while you use Windows. WinPong comes with optional sound effects that you can hear when the ball hits the screen edges or the mouse pointer. You can use the mouse pointer as a paddle to involve yourself in this program's entertaining activities.

.running the program

As soon as you run WinPong, the bouncing ball appears and begins to travel around your Windows desktop. There are default values

◘ This bouncing ball won't break windows.

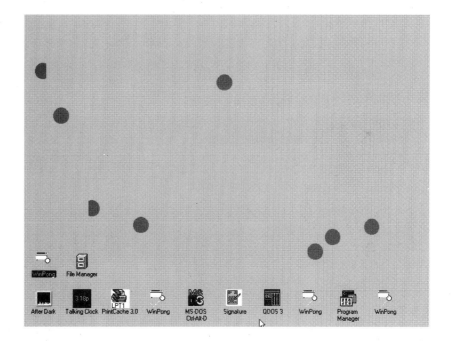

for a variety of settings, but you will probably want to set your own preferences. To do so, click on the WinPong icon to display the System Menu.

You can also control when the ringing sound is made. If you want no sound at all, choose Off. If you want the sound to be made only when the ball bounces away from the mouse pointer, or "cursor," choose Upon Hitting Cursor. If you want sound effects whenever the bouncing ball hits the mouse paddle or the screen edges, choose Upon Hitting Edges & Cursor from the Sound submenu.

Once you've set the controls to the values you enjoy most, save your settings by choosing Save Settings.

◻ ◻ ◻ ◻ ◻ ◻ ◻ ◻ ◻ ◻ ◻ ◻ ◻ ◻ ◻ ◻ behind the trick

Eric Saito wrote this enjoyable little freeware program while he was a student at the University of Hawaii. Mail I sent to him was returned, so I don't know his address. If you know how to get in touch with Eric, drop me a line. I'll update this section of the book for later editions.

WinRoach

the big picture

WinRoach (WINROACH.EXE) is an entertaining Windows 3.0 and
3.1 program that scatters roaches everywhere. They scurry across
the screen and hide under windows. When they get in your way,
use mouse button 1 to squash and exterminate them. This latest
version comes with a wandering roaches option. Roaches wander
out from behind windows while you just sit back and watch!

running the program

This entertaining program makes closing and moving windows a
treat. Why? Because every time you close or move a window, you

■ Use the mouse to squash those little buggers.

may expose a roach, who, like a real roach, runs and hides. Specifically, the roaches scurry behind the next active window. Or, if they find another window to hide under on the way to the active window, they hide under that one.

As an added treat, the roaches wander out from the windows they are hiding behind. They run to the edge of the desktop and scurry back under a window. When the desktop is completely covered with windows, the roaches can't wander very far.

Just like real roaches, they can be stepped on. Just position the mouse pointer over the roach—if you can catch it—and click mouse button 1. If you hit a roach, you'll know it. You'll see a visual Splat!

Hidden roaches make no impact on system performance, so you can afford to run this program and keep things exciting when you close or move windows. If wandering roaches start to impact system performance, simply decrease the frequency to make the roaches wander less frequently.

When you start WinRoach you will see the WinRoach icon. No window is associated with this program. Soon a number of roaches—four is the default—appear randomly on the desktop. When a roach is exposed, it will scurry toward the active window or icon. As time goes on you will notice several roaches wandering across the desktop.

You can change various parameters with the menu items that appear in the Control Menu. To bring up this menu, position the mouse pointer over the WinRoach icon and click on mouse button 1. The WinRoach menu items are:

- **Add Roach** creates another roach and places it at random on the desktop. You can add up to 10 roaches.

- **Delete Roach** deletes a roach from the desktop. It randomly picks which roach to delete.

- **Options** brings up the WinRoach dialog box so you can set the various options.

- **ReScatter** scatters the roaches over the desktop. Use this option if you want to find the roaches without closing or moving your windows.

- **About** brings up the About Box dialog for WinRoach.

With WinRoach's Options dialog box you can set various parameters that are used to start up WinRoach and to run the program. These option values are stored in a WINROACH.INI file that is created in your WINDOWS directory

▪ behind the trick

WinRoach is definitely entertaining. You'll get an enormous satisfaction from squashing these pseudo bugs. And this program has no adverse environmental impact—you needn't worry about overpopulation, underpopulation, or food-chain ramifications.

WinRoach is a shareware product and is available free of charge for a period of 30 days. If you intend to use this product, you should register WinRoach. The base registration fee is $12.95. For an additional $5.00 for shipping and handling, you will receive a diskette containing a registered version of WinRoach and its source code. Register by sending the registration form (found at the bottom of the WINROACH.DOC file) to

New Generation Software
P.O. Box 9700
Dept. 271
Austin, TX 78766
(713) 283-6760
(800) 964-7638 (orders)
(512) 388-4053 (FAX)
Compuserve: 70312,127

Go ahead. Bug these people.

t r i c k 61 ♠

Wywo

The WYWO (WYWO.EXE) program is a telephone message system like the familiar pink "While You Were Out" note pads. The program manages phone messages for groups of users and can be used on both stand-alone DOS computers and a variety of network installations.

WYWO lets you send messages to other users, store incoming messages on-file, paste messages to the Clipboard, and print messages.

■ No more piles of pink message slips accumulating on your desk.

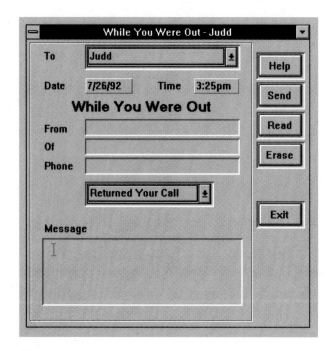

You can even use passwords to protect other users from reading your messages.

Prior to using the program, you must run the WSETUP.EXE program from the SYBEX\WYWO directory to create the necessary internal entries for desired user names and directories. Only then can you run the program from within Windows.

WSETUP.EXE is the administration program for WYWO. It is used to set up all of the user names and directories for the WYWO system. It also clears user's passwords if they have forgotten them. WSETUP creates a file called WYWO.DAT in the directory dedicated for the WYWO system. You will be asked for the directory's full path at the start of WSETUP. Once you enter it, you will be able to add, modify, or delete users in the WYWO.DAT file of the specified directory.

To add a user, click on the Add button and fill in the name of the new user. Click on OK to enter the name into the system. You can modify the user's name or clear the user's password in one of two ways. Either click on the Modify button after you've clicked on the user name to be modified, or double-click on the user name itself. Then you can change the user's name or clear the user's password. To delete a user, select the user's name and click on the Delete button. Click on the Exit button when all users have been added. You are now ready to run WYWO.

running the WYWO program

When you run WYWO for the first time on a workstation or on a stand-alone PC, you wll be asked for the path where the WYWO.DAT file can be found. Use the file selector to search and locate the previously created WYWO.DAT file and then select it to continue. You'll find the path of the WYWO.DAT file in the Windows WIN.INI file of each workstation. Once the WYWO sheet is on-screen, you are ready to send and receive telephone messages.

sending phone messages

Before you can send a phone message, you must fill in all the appropriate fields on the message sheet. After that, click on the Send button. If no user has been selected to receive the phone message, the user list will drop down. Select a user and click on the Send button again.

To select a user, click on the down arrow in the To field to see a list of user names. Next, click on the user name you want. Use the scroll bar and the ↑ or ↓ keys to display user names that you can't see.

To select a message, click on the down arrow in the message type field to see the message types. Next, click on the message type you want. Use the scroll bar and the up and down arrows to display message types you can't see.

reading phone messages

To read phone messages in Edit mode, click on the Read button. If no user is currently active, select an "active" user whose messages you want to read. Next, click on the message selector to select the message you want to read. Click on the right side to move forward through the messages, or click on the left side to move backward. You can also select messages by moving the center slider bar.

After you've read the messages, clear the message sheet by clicking on the Erase button while you are still in Edit mode. If you want to quit WYWO, click on the Exit button.

To read old phone messages, click on the Old button. The Old button is enabled if there are old messages to read. If not, you can't click on the Old button.

behind the trick

The shareware version of WYWO is provided for limited use, for evaluation purposes only. If you make use of WYWO and would like the commercial Version 2.0, which doesn't have the shareware screen and includes the complete printed documentation, you can order it for a fee of $69.95.

Caliente
2594-96 Berlin Turnpike
Suite 201
Newington, CT 06111
(203) 667-2159
FAX: (203) 665-7382

Solution to Magic Trick 48, the Button Madness Program

To keep you from reading this solution before you actually try the Button Madness program, it is printed in "mirror print." In other words, you have to hold this page before a mirror in order to read the solution below.

In any order you like, you must click (once only) on each of the sixteen squares.

about the author

Judd Robbins is the *Windows Tips* conference coordinator and a weekly columnist for the Windows On Line Bulletin Board System. He is the best-selling author of more than fifteen books on operating systems and software, including *Mastering DOS 5* and *Supercharging Windows*, both from SYBEX.

Help Yourself with
Another Quality Sybex Book

Mastering Windows 3.1
Robert Cowart

The complete guide to installing, using, and making the most of Windows on IBM PCs and compatibles now in an up-to-date new edition. Part I provides detailed, hands-on coverage of major Windows features that are essential for day-to-day use. Part II offers complete tutorials on the accessory programs. Part III explores a selection of advanced topics.

600pp; 7 1/2" x 9"
ISBN: 0-89588-842-4

Available
at Better
Bookstores
Everywhere

Sybex Inc.
2021 Challenger Drive
Alameda, CA 94501
Telephone (800) 227-2346
Fax (510) 523-2373

Sybex. Help Yourself.

Help Yourself with
Another Quality Sybex Book

Windows 3.1
Instant Reference
Marshall L. Moseley

Enjoy fast access to concise information on every Windows 3.1 mouse and keyboard command, including the accessory programs and Help facilities. Perfect for any Windows 3.1 user who needs an occasional on-the-job reminder.

262pp; 4 3/4" x 8"
ISBN: 0-89588-844-0

Available
at Better
Bookstores
Everywhere

Sybex Inc.
2021 Challenger Drive
Alameda, CA 94501
Telephone (800) 227-2346
Fax (510) 523-2373

Sybex. Help Yourself.

Help Yourself with
Another Quality Sybex Book

Supercharging Windows
Judd Robbins

Here's a gold mine of answers to common questions, with details on undocumented features, optimization, and advanced capabilities. This book's wide-ranging topics include Windows for laptops, programming language interfacing, memory-resident software, and networking—just to name a few. Includes two disks full of productivity tools, utilities, games, and accessories.

1011pp; 71/2" x9"
ISBN: 0-89588-862-9

Available
at Better
Bookstores
Everywhere

Sybex Inc.
2021 Challenger Drive
Alameda, CA 94501
Telephone (800) 227-2346
Fax (510) 523-2373

Sybex. Help Yourself.

Help Yourself with
Another Quality Sybex Book

Mastering Microsoft Word for Windows,

Version 2.0

Second Edition

Michael J. Young

Here is an up-to-date new edition of our complete guide to Word for Windows, featuring the latest software release. It offers a tutorial for newcomers, and hands-on coverage of intermediate to advanced topicswith desktop publishing skills emphasized. Special topics include: tables and columns, fonts, graphics, Styles and Templates, macros, and multiple windows.

596pp; 7 1/2" x 9"
ISBN: 0-7821-1012-6

Available
at Better
Bookstores
Everywhere

Sybex Inc.
2021 Challenger Drive
Alameda, CA 94501
Telephone (800) 227-2346
Fax (510) 523-2373

SYBEX

Sybex. Help Yourself.

SYBEX

FREE BROCHURE!

Complete this form today, and we'll send you a full-color brochure of Sybex bestsellers.

Please supply the name of the Sybex book purchased.

_____

How would you rate it?

_____ Excellent   _____ Very Good   _____ Average   _____ Poor

Why did you select this particular book?

_____ Recommended to me by a friend
_____ Recommended to me by store personnel
_____ Saw an advertisement in _____
_____ Author's reputation
_____ Saw in Sybex catalog
_____ Required textbook
_____ Sybex reputation
_____ Read book review in _____
_____ In-store display
_____ Other _____

Where did you buy it?

_____ Bookstore
_____ Computer Store or Software Store
_____ Catalog (name: _____)
_____ Direct from Sybex
_____ Other: _____

Did you buy this book with your personal funds?

_____ Yes   _____ No

About how many computer books do you buy each year?

_____ 1-3   _____ 3-5   _____ 5-7   _____ 7-9   _____ 10+

About how many Sybex books do you own?

_____ 1-3   _____ 3-5   _____ 5-7   _____ 7-9   _____ 10+

Please indicate your level of experience with the software covered in this book:

_____ Beginner   _____ Intermediate   _____ Advanced

Which types of software packages do you use regularly?

_____ Accounting	_____ Databases	_____ Networks
_____ Amiga	_____ Desktop Publishing	_____ Operating Systems
_____ Apple/Mac	_____ File Utilities	_____ Spreadsheets
_____ CAD	_____ Money Management	_____ Word Processing
_____ Communications	_____ Languages	_____ Other _____
		(please specify)

Which of the following best describes your job title?

____ Administrative/Secretarial   ____ President/CEO

____ Director   ____ Manager/Supervisor

____ Engineer/Technician   ____ Other _____
                                                                          (please specify)

Comments on the weaknesses/strengths of this book: _____

_____

_____

_____

_____

Name _____

Street _____

City/State/Zip _____

Phone _____

PLEASE FOLD, SEAL, AND MAIL TO SYBEX

SYBEX INC.
Department M
2021 CHALLENGER DR.
ALAMEDA, CALIFORNIA USA
94501

SYBEX

SEAL

Windows Magic Tricks

Installation of Disk

For installation instructions, please refer to the Introduction.

Copy Protection

None of the programs on the disk is copy-protected. However, in all cases, reselling these programs without authorization is expressly forbidden.

If you need a 3½-inch disk ...

To receive a 3½-inch disk, please return the orginal 5¼-inch disk with a written request to:

SYBEX Inc.
Customer Service Department
2021 Challenger Drive
Alameda, CA 94501
(800) 227-2346
Fax: (510) 523-2373

Be sure to include your name, complete mailing address, and the following reference number: 1119-X. Otherwise, your request cannot be processed. Allow six weeks for delivery.

If your disk is defective...

To obtain a replacement disk, please refer to the instructions outlined on the warranty page at the front of the book.